GUIDE TO ROOF AND GUTTER INSTALLATION AND REPAIR

McGraw-Hill Paperbacks
Home Improvement Series

GUIDE TO ROOF AND GUTTER INSTALLATION AND REPAIR

McGRAW-HILL BOOK COMPANY

New York   St. Louis   San Francisco   Auckland   Bogotá   Düsseldorf
Johannesburg   London   Madrid   Mexico   Montreal   New Delhi   Panama
Paris   São Paulo   Singapore   Sydney   Tokyo   Toronto

1 2 3 4 5 6 7 8 9 0 SMSM 8 3 2 1 0

Library of Congress Cataloging in Publication Data

Main entry under title:

Guide to roof and gutter installation and repair.

  (McGraw-Hill paperbacks home improvement series)
  Originally issued (c1976) by the Hardware-Paint
Trades Division of the Minnesota Mining and Manufacturing
Company under title: The home pro roofs and gutters
guide.
  1. Roofs — Amateurs' manuals. 2. Gutters — Amateurs'
manuals. I. Minnesota Mining and Manufacturing Company.
Hardware-Paint Trades Division. The home pro roofs and
gutters guide.
TH2401.G84   695   79-13954
ISBN 0-07-045974-6

Cover photo showing three-dimensional asphalt shingles
courtesy of Asphalt Roofing Manufacturers Association.

Contents

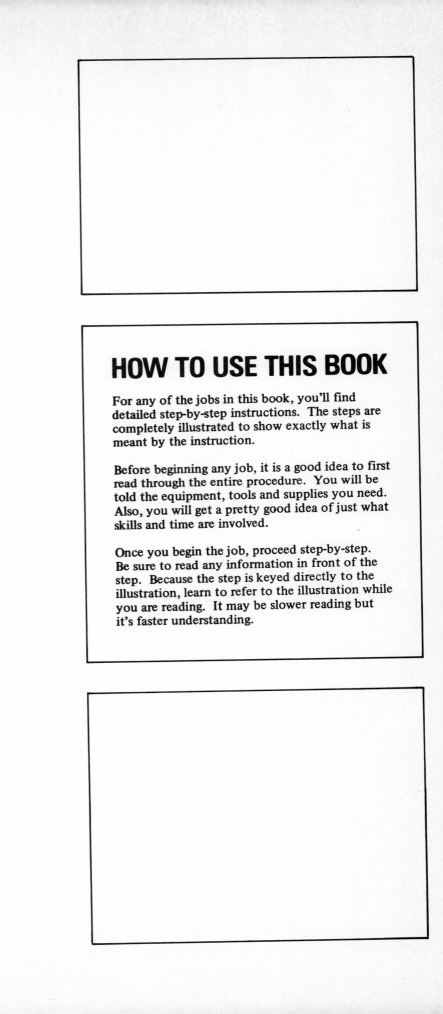

HOW TO USE THIS BOOK

For any of the jobs in this book, you'll find detailed step-by-step instructions. The steps are completely illustrated to show exactly what is meant by the instruction.

Before beginning any job, it is a good idea to first read through the entire procedure. You will be told the equipment, tools and supplies you need. Also, you will get a pretty good idea of just what skills and time are involved.

Once you begin the job, proceed step-by-step. Be sure to read any information in front of the step. Because the step is keyed directly to the illustration, learn to refer to the illustration while you are reading. It may be slower reading but it's faster understanding.

GUIDE TO ROOF AND GUTTER INSTALLATION AND REPAIR

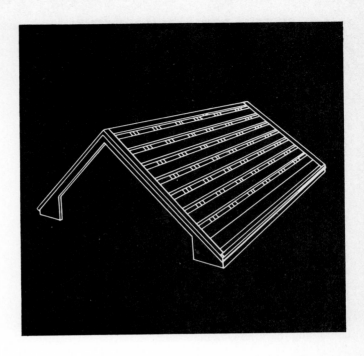

ROOFING PREPARATIONS

1

Roofing materials are designed to seal the roof and protect the house from damage. The term roofing materials [1] applies to all materials installed above the roof sheathing [2].

Many roofing materials can be replaced or repaired with professional results by almost anyone willing to plan carefully and work slowly. However, some roofing jobs require professional help and are so indicated in the appropriate instructions.

This book shows how to **replace** existing roofing materials with one of the following materials:

Strip form asphalt shingles
Individual asphalt shingles
Wooden shingles
Shakes
Mineral surfaced roll roofing

This book also shows how to **repair** existing roofs containing the following materials:

Strip form asphalt shingles
Individual asphalt shingles
Wooden shingles
Shakes
Asbestos cement shingles
Mineral surfaced roll roofing
Rock and gravel roofing

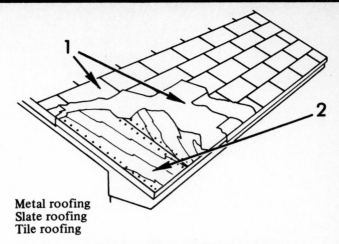

Metal roofing
Slate roofing
Tile roofing

The roofing materials, as well as sheathing, other materials required for roofing, and general safety are described in the following pages:

▶ **Roofing Surface Materials**

The term roofing surface materials as used in this book refers to the external roof covering and does not include flashing [1] or drip edges [3]. Flashings prevent leaks where roofing surfaces meet chimneys [2] and other roofing surfaces. Drip edges guide water away from roof edges and fascia boards [4]. Many different types of roofing surface materials are available from building supply stores.

The type of roofing surface material to install is limited by the local fire codes, roof pitch, and strength of the roof.

Some roofing surface materials, such as decorative rock and gravel, are suitable only for low pitch or flat roofs while others, such as slate or tile, are heavy and require a strong supporting roof frame. In some areas, wooden shingles and shakes are prohibited by local fire codes.

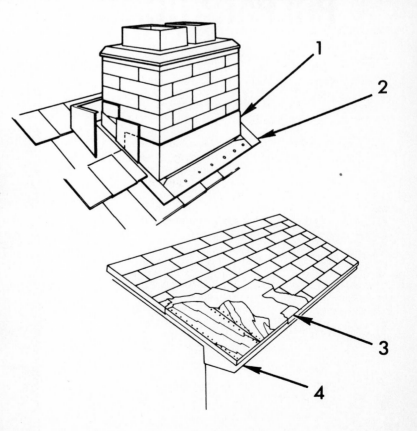

Asphalt shingles are available in strip form or individual shingles in several attractive patterns and colors. They are made from felt saturated with asphalt and coated with mineral granules. They are relatively inexpensive, are fire resistant and make a durable roofing surface.

Asbestos cement shingles, sometimes called mineral fiber shingles, are available in several shapes and colors that make them similar to shakes or asphalt shingles. They are fireproof and make a very durable roofing surface. They are much heavier than shakes or asphalt shingles. The roof framing may have to be reinforced to support the extra weight.

Wooden shingles are usually made from redwood, red cedar, or cypress woods. Shingles are graded No. 1 or No. 2, with No. 1 being the better shingle. Unless treated, they offer little or no fire resistance. Some local fire codes restrict their use. However, they are still used because they make an attractive roof.

Shakes are thick wooden shingles made from the same woods as wooden shingles. They are hand split and therefore much more rustic in appearance than wooden shingles. They are slightly more durable than wooden shingles but are much more expensive.

Mineral surface roll roofing is roofing paper that has been coated with asphalt and mineral granules. It is available in several attractive colors. It is a less durable surface material than asphalt shingles.

Decorative rock and gravel is applied to tar paper covered roofs to improve appearance and durability. It is more fire resistant than asphalt shingles.

Metal roofs are seldom used for houses. Replacing a metal roof takes at least a two-man crew and special equipment.

Slate or tile roofs are very durable and fireproof. They are very heavy and require a roof frame designed to carry the extra weight.

Roofs covered with slate or tile rarely require replacing. Since slate or tile is much heavier than other roofing surface materials, it is recommended that a building contractor be used to install these materials. He will insure that the existing building structure is capable of carrying the heavy weight.

▶ **Other Materials Required for Roofing**

Sheathing

Roofing surface materials are nailed or stapled to the sheathing. Sheathing can be either solid [1] or open [2]. It will depend on the type of roofing surface material used.

Solid sheathing [1] is made of plywood or boards laid side by side. When solid sheathing is made from boards, it is best to use tongue and groove boards because they stay flat. If the sheathing boards are wider than 6 inches, they tend to curl. Curled boards don't provide the smooth surface needed by roofing surface materials. Thus, always use boards with a width of 6 inches or less.

Open sheathing [2] is made by laying narrow boards parallel to one another with a 1 or 2 inch space between the boards. Wooden shingles and shakes are applied to open sheathing. Open sheathing allows the bottom surfaces of shingles and shakes to dry more rapidly than they would if attached to solid sheathing. Other types of roofing surface materials are attached to solid sheathing.

If sheathing is defective, it must be replaced before a new roofing surface is put on.

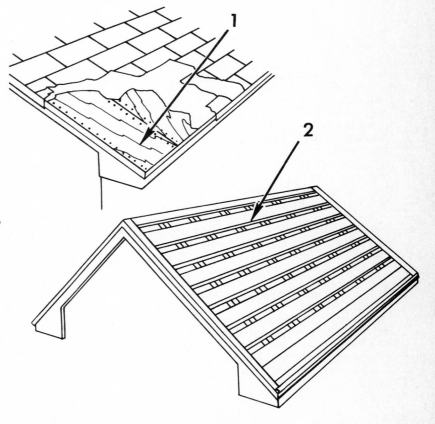

Underlayments

Some roofs have an underlayment [1] between
the sheathing and the roofing surface material.
The underlayment reduces air flow through the
shingling and protects shingling from any
sheathing resins.

The underlayment should allow water vapor
between the layers of roofing to evaporate. Other-
wise, moisture or frost can collect between the
underlayment and the sheathing. This moisture
can cause the sheathing to decay or be attacked by
fungus. For these reasons very heavy felts are not
used as underlayments. Also, underlayments are
impregnated with, but not coated with, asphalt.

Underlayments consist of dry felts, saturated felts
or heavy paper made of organic or asbestos fibers
impregnated with asphalt. They are purchased in
roll form. Heavy felts impregnated with asphalt
are usually called tar paper or building paper. Tar
paper rolls [2] are usually 36 inches wide and
weigh 15 to 30 pounds per square.

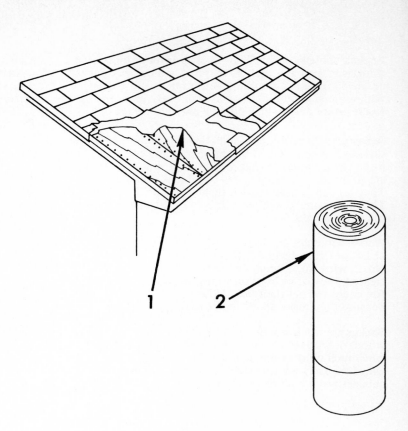

Flashing

Flashing materials are used around chimneys [3]
and vents [4], in valleys [1], at ridges [2] and at
the edges [5] of roofing surfaces. Flashings prevent water from leaking into a house at the joints
between the roofing surfaces and the joints
between roofing surfaces and other adjacent
building surfaces.

Flashings may be made from the same type of
material as the roofing surface or from other more
durable materials. Chimney flashings are
made from metal pieces. Valley flashings are
usually made of metal for wooden shingled and
shake roofing. Valley flashings for composition
roofing are often made from composition
materials. Flashings at eaves [6] and at ridges [2]
are generally made of composition materials.

It is important to avoid incompatible combina-
tions of roofing surfacing materials and flashing
materials or attachments. Incompatibilities can
result in the corrosion of attachments or parts of
the flashing materials. Material compatibility is
considered in the sections on installing the various
roofing surfacing materials.

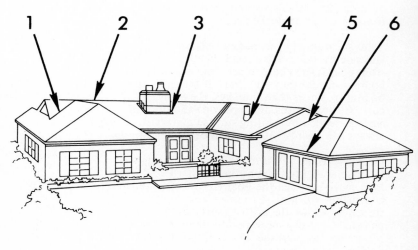

Drip edges [1] are usually made of metal strips. They are installed below the roofing surface material and bent down over the edges of the roof.

Gravel stops [2] are made by bending the drip edge material up into a ridge along the edge of a roof. This reduces the likelihood that gravel will blow off of a rock and gravel roof.

Roofing is fastened to sheathing with roofing nails [3], common nails [4], or staples [5]. Staples are usually used for asphalt shingles. Roofing nails have large diameter heads and are used with asphalt shingles and roll roofing. Common nails are used for wooden shingles, shakes and asbestos cement (mineral fiber) shingles.

Roofing nails are galvanized (zinc coated). Sometimes copper nails are used for attaching copper flashings. Galvanized roofing nails are sometimes used with lead washers to prevent electrochemical action on metal roofs. The sizes of roofing nails range in length from 3/4 to 2 inches and have 3/8 inch diameter heads.

Common nails are generally the 6 penny size or greater and 2 inches long or longer.

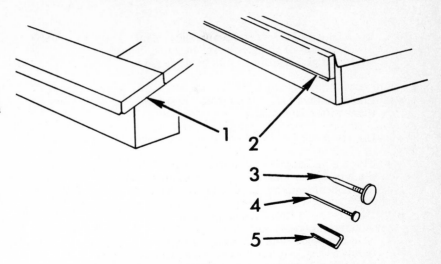

Staples are 1 inch wide and range in length from 1/2 to 1-1/4 inches.

There are a number of **sealers** and **cements** used for roofing work. The proper roofing cement for mineral-surfaced roll roofing is usually packaged with the roofing paper. **Read the instructions on the can carefully.** If you are still unsure of the proper sealer or cement for your roofing work, ask your supplier.

GENERAL SAFETY RULES

Working safety on the roof depends basically on the following general safety rules:

- Avoid working on a roof in bad weather.

- Do not work on a wet roof.

- Wear rubber-soled shoes.

- Keep your work area clean so you won't trip on anything.

- Do not try to lift a two-man load alone. Get help lifting heavy objects.

- Do not unbundle shingles until you are ready to use them. They may be blown about by a gust of wind.

- Avoid contact with electrical power lines.

- Check whether the roof will support the weight of the new roofing materials and the roofers. When in doubt, get professional advice.

- Do not place very heavy loads on any single area of the roof. Distribute the bundles [1] of shingles or rolls of roofing paper across the entire roof.

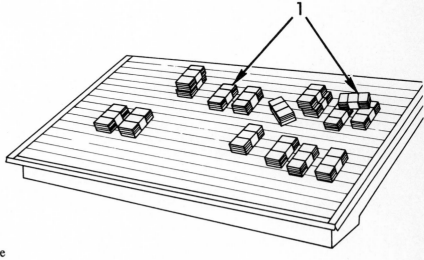

- Do not attempt to put a heavy tile or slate roof onto framing that was designed for shingling or roll roofing.

GENERAL SAFETY RULES

- Use adequate ladders and scaffolding. The lower courses of shingles, eaves flashing, drip edges and gravel stops should be done from scaffolding.

- Check ladders for soundness before using them with a heavy load.

- Use sturdy braces [1] to hold rung ladders [2] or chicken ladders [4] on roofing surfaces. This is especially important for roofs with pitch of 1/3 or greater. On wooden shingled roofs, cleats may be used instead of ladders.

- Use cleats [5] for added safety when pitch of wooden-shingled roofs is 1/3 or greater. A cleat is a board which is attached to a roof. It acts as a step to prevent you from slipping. Method of installing cleat is described on Page 48.

- Place ladders so that you won't have to lean away from the ladder to work.

- Always keep your hips between the ladder rails [3] when reaching out.

- When reaching out, always hold ladder with the other hand.

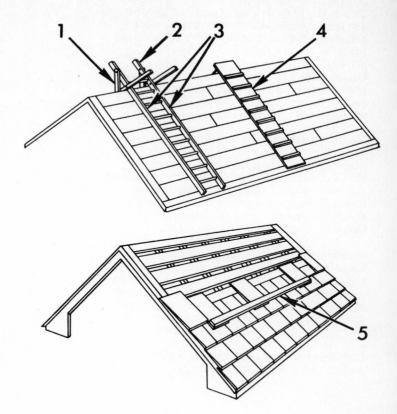

- Use the proper tools to remove nails and shingles. The use of rippers and nail pullers is described on Page 73.

- Use small seats [1] for both yourself and materials except when working on roofs with a very low pitch. Pitch is described on Page 7.

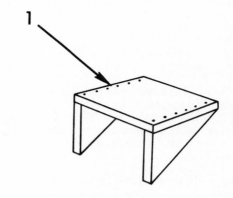

Selecting materials for replacing roofing is easier when you know the available options. Usually, roofing can be replaced with the same type of materials as those that were on the roof.

Before changing to other materials, a number of factors must be considered. These include:

- Will the new materials be weather-proof when installed on a roof with the existing pitch?

- Are the color, size and pattern in harmony with other architectural features?

- Can the existing framing support the anticipated weight of the roofing and the roofers?

- How difficult will it be to install the new materials?

- What will be the cost of the materials?

▶ **Pitch**

The pitch of a roof restricts the selection of roofing materials and how they are applied. The

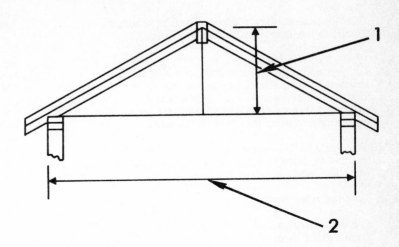

pitch indicates the incline of a roof as the ratio of the rise [1] to the total span [2] of the roof. It is expressed as a fraction. For example: if the rise is 6 feet and the span is 24 feet, the pitch is 6/24 or 1/4. As the roof gets steeper, the fraction becomes larger (e.g., 1/4 is steeper than 1/5, which is steeper than 1/6).

Pitch

Do not confuse pitch of a roof with slope of a roof. The slope of a roof is defined as the ratio of the rise [2] to the run [1]. You can see that the run is not the same length as the span [3].

Any material can be used on a high-pitched roof. For lower pitched roofs you are limited in your choice of materials. If the pitch of your roof is 1/6 or less, you are limited to using composition roll roofing, decorative rock and gravel on hot mopped layers of tar paper, or a roof built up of hot mopped layers of tar paper. Of these three types, you can install only composition roll roofing without professional help.

With a low-pitched roof, the wind could drive water up under wooden shingles, shakes, asbestos cement shingles, or asphalt shingles. For this reason, wooden shingles, shakes and asbestos cement shingles are seldom used for a pitch less than 1/5.

Asphalt shingles lie flatter than wooden or asbestos cement shingles and may be used on a roof with a pitch as low as 1/6.

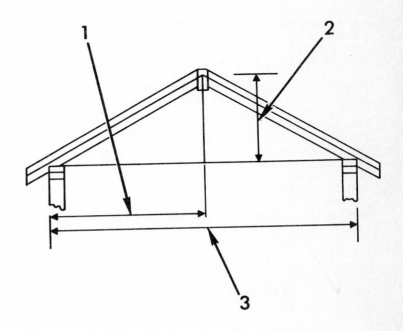

SELECTING MATERIALS

▶ Color, Size, and Pattern

Selecting color, size, and pattern of new roofing surface materials is a matter of personal choice.

If you live in a warm area, you may wish to choose light-colored materials to reflect the sun's heat. A sample of the new roofing surface material should be compared with the coloring of brick chimneys and brick walls, or other not so easy to change colors, to preserve color harmony and attractiveness of the house.

The size and pattern of new shingling should be compatible with the existing architecture. Very large shingles may look bad on a very small house.

▶ Existing Roof Framing

It is necessary to consider whether the existing roof framing can support different roofing surface materials. It is very possible that roof framing originally covered with roll roofing, asphalt shingles, wooden shingles, or shake shingles will not be able to support a covering of asbestos cement shingles, slate, or tile without additional reinforcing.

Existing roof framing normally can support a new covering of the same materials over existing materials without reinforcement. This does not apply to slate, tile, or asbestos cement roofing.

▶ Difficulty of Installation

Replacing certain roofing surface materials requires special equipment, skills, and experience. Examples of such materials are decorative rock and gravel on hot mopped layers of tar, a roof surface built up of hot mopped layers of tar paper, metal roofing, and slate or tile roofing. Since it is difficult to replace these roofing surface materials, it should be done by a professional roofer.

Hot mopping is a fire hazard and requires special equipment and protective clothing. You need experience to avoid applying a coating which is too hot or too cold. If the asphalt is too hot, its quality as a binder will be impaired and it may burn the felt. Also, the layers of asphalt will be too thin and will crack. If the asphalt is too cold, the layer will be too thick. This uses too much material and increases the cost.

Metal roofing is not widely used in residential construction. The metal sheets are too large and difficult to handle.

Slate or tile roofing surface materials are heavy. Two or more persons are required to replace slate or tile roofs.

▬ ESTIMATING ROOFING MATERIAL ▬

You can determine total square footage of roofing by measuring the rectangle A-1, trapezoids A-2, A-3, and A-4 and triangle A-5 shapes of the roof surfaces, calculating the areas, and adding the calculated areas together. All roofs contain at least one or more of these shapes.

Measure the roof surfaces along the eaves [2,4], ridges [3], and gabled edges [1,5]. In many cases exact square footage is not needed. Thus, the measurements and calculations can be simplified. For example, treat roof surfaces A-1 and A-2 as equal rectangles. Also, treat the surfaces A-3 and A-4 as equal rectangles of shortened lengths. When using this simplified method, you may initially buy less surface material than you need. However, when you have installed this material, you will know the amount of additional material needed.

All roofing surface materials are sold by the square. A square of roofing will cover 100 square feet of roofing area. The number of squares of roofing you will need can be determined by dividing the total square footage of the roofs by 100.

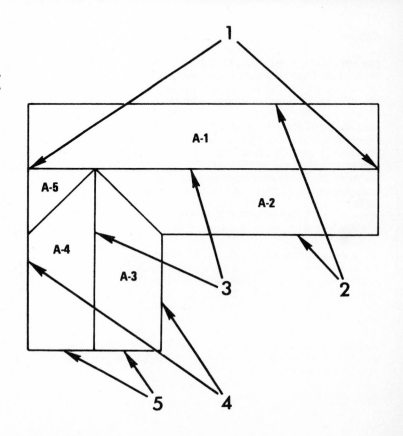

The total costs to replace your roof include the cost of the roofing surface materials, as well as nails, roof coatings, plastic roof cements, flashing materials, equipment rentals, allowance for replacing wooden boards at the edges of the roof and for repairing any damaged sheathing. However, the cost of the roofing surface materials and underlayment is so much greater than the combined costs of the other items that a reasonable estimate of the cost to replace your roofing will be the cost of the roofing surface materials and underlayment.

Therefore, to estimate the cost of replacing your roofing, use the following procedure. It will give you a slightly low estimate, but should be close enough to meet your needs.

1. Determine the number of squares of roofing surface material and underlayment needed to cover your roofs.

2. Go to a building supply store in your neighborhood and obtain the cost per square of the roofing surface materials and underlayment you are planning to install.

3. Multiply the number of squares needed by the price per square to obtain your cost.

4. If desired, you can now make a good comparison of the cost of alternate roofing surface materials.

PREPARING THE ROOF

This book does not provide instructions to replace slate or tile shingles, or rock and gravel roofing. However, instructions are provided to remove these materials. After these materials have been removed, they can be replaced with one of the easier-to-apply materials for which installation instructions are given.

Before installing a new roofing surface material, the surface of the existing roof must be prepared. The procedures described on Pages 10-26 show how to prepare the roof.

WARNING

Be sure to review the general safety rules before starting.

PREPARING THE ROOF

▶ **Tools and Supplies**

The following tools and supplies are needed to remove old roofing and to prepare a roof for new roofing:

- A shingle ripper [1] to remove shingles and the nails that hold them in place.

- A pry bar [2] to assist in removing any sheathing which must be replaced.

- A chisel [3] to remove shingles and trim sheathing that is to be repaired or replaced.

- A flat-surfaced spade [4] to pry off old shingles.

- A hook-nosed roofing knife [5] to cut out old roofing paper and to cut new paper to size.

- A hammer [6] for replacing boards, strips, shingles, and composition roofing paper.

- 15 lb felt roofing paper for underlayment.

- Flashing material to replace existing flashings.

- Asphalt roofing cement and roofing lap cement to install composition roll roofing.

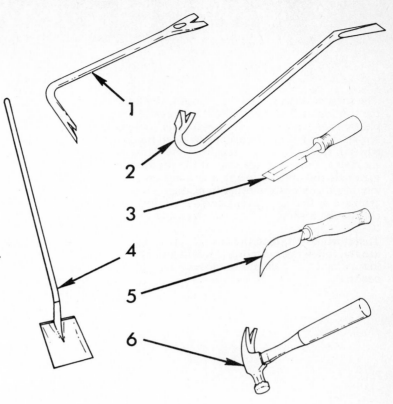

- A shingling hatchet [1] to split shingles and to remove shingles.

- A chalk line and reel [2] to mark straight lines across roofing surfaces and along valley flashings.

- Extension ladders [3], ladder-type scaffold hooks [6], and scaffold board [7] to permit carrying materials onto roof and for installing eaves flashing strips, starter strips and the first few courses of shingles.

- A folding rule [4] and a steel tape [5] for measuring roofing paper and locating chalk lines.

- Replacement sheathing and wooden trim as required to replace damaged and decayed items.

- Roofing nails and common nails to replace flashings and defective sheathing or wooden trim.

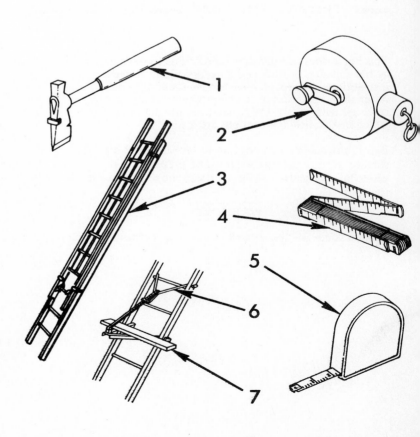

▶ **Remove Roofing Surface Materials**

Use this procedure to remove all types of roofing surface materials except metal roofing.

WARNING

Keep clear of electrical power lines and television aerials that attach to roof. Electrical shock and injury could result.

When working on a roof with a pitch greater than 1/4, use small seats [1] for yourself and for materials to avoid injury from falls.

Use care when you remove roofing surface material near chimneys and valleys. There is flashing material under the roofing surface material. You should use the old flashing material as a pattern to cut new flashing. A pattern will save you time and trouble when measuring and cutting new flashing.

Use care when removing roofing surface materials from sheathing. If sheathing is cracked or broken while removing roofing materials, it will have to be replaced. Damage to sheathing will increase your work and costs.

Remove Composition and Built-up Roofing Surface Materials

Composition roll roofing, hot asphalt or tar mopped layers of roofing paper, and decorative rock and gravel roofing are removed in the following manner:

1. Using roofing knife, cut through the old roofing surface material at one edge of the roof.

2. Place shingle ripper or similar prying tool through cut and remove old roofing surface material.

For removing other types of roofing surface materials, go to next section (below).

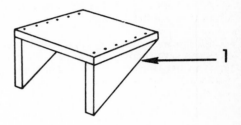

Remove Other Types of Roofing Surface Materials

1. Carefully remove roofing surface materials [1] and flashing [2] from ridges and hips. Do not break or damage ridge or hip boards [3].

When removing roofing surface materials near chimneys and valleys, try not to damage flashing [6,7]. You will need the old flashing to use as a pattern.

2. Remove the rest of the roofing surface materials [5] and underlayment [4] from the roof.

3. Remove all nails or staples used to fasten roofing materials to sheathing.

The next few pages show how to replace or repair various items on the roof. Review the instructions and use those which apply to your particular roof.

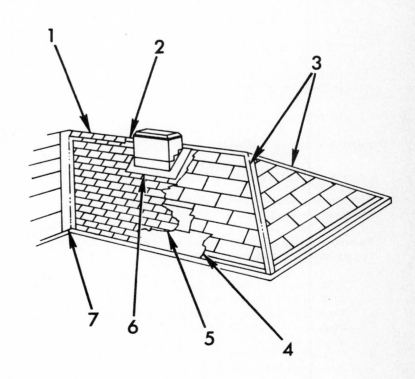

▶ **Remove Valley Flashings**

Valleys are places where two roofing surfaces meet. Valley flashing [2] may be made of metal or composition roofing material. Metal flashing is usually installed over a 36 inch wide strip of composition roofing material.

Composition roofing is usually installed as valley flashing in two layers. There is usually a 36 inch wide strip cemented over an 18 inch wide strip. The flashing is also cemented to the drip edge.

When removing the flashings, try not to damage the top [1] and bottom [3] vees. You will need them to use as a pattern to cut new flashing.

1.   Remove nails and pry the flashing away from drip edge and sheathing.

2.   Using roofing knife, cut off top and bottom vees and save them to use as patterns when you cut new flashings. The other pieces of flashing are not needed.

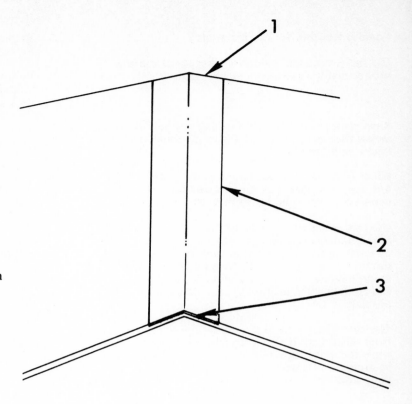

▶ **Remove Eaves Flashing and Drip Edges**

Eaves flashing is made from composition roofing material. It is cemented to the drip edges [3] and nailed to the sheathing.

1.   Remove eaves flashing [1] and underlayment [2].

2.   Remove drip edges [3].

▶ **Remove Chimney Flashings**

CAUTION

The chimney flashing should always be replaced when resurfacing a roof.

Remove flashing carefully. It will be needed as a pattern to cut new materials.

1.   Using chisel and small sledge hammer, carefully remove the sealing mortar [4] along the top of the cap flashing. Use a brush to clean away loose mortar and dust.

2.   Carefully pull the cap flashing pieces [5] away from the chimney using two small pry bars. Keep the pieces to use as patterns for the new flashing.

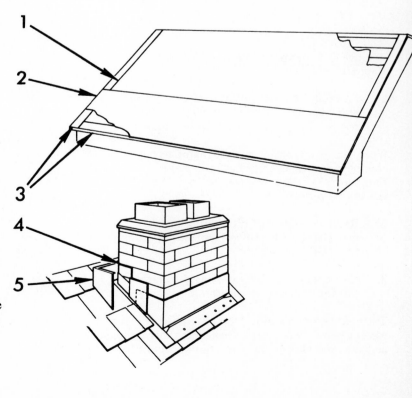

3. Remove nails that attach base flashing [1] to sheathing.

4. Carefully pull base flashing pieces away from sheathing and chimney. Keep the pieces as patterns for new flashing.

5. Check chimney mortar joints for loose or missing mortar. If mortar needs to be repaired, your roofing material supplier can provide materials and instructions.

6. Remove all old loose roofing material debris. Clean chimney bricks and exposed sheathing with a brush.

▶ **Remove Vent Pipe Flashing**

Vent pipe flashing [3] should be replaced. It is inexpensive and is available from most building suppliers as preformed flashing and ready to install.

1. Scrape old roofing cement [2] away from flashing on vent.

2. Remove nails and pry flashing away from sheathing. Remove flashing by pulling up over vent stack.

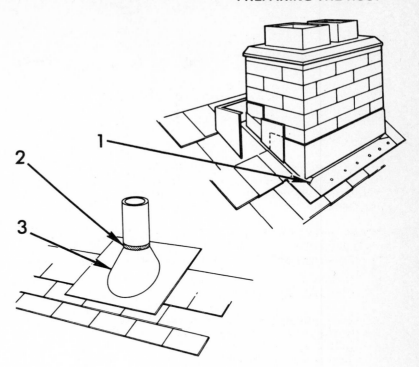

3. Using putty knife and wire brush, remove roofing cement from vent stack and sheathing.

▶ **Remove Flashings Where Roofs Meet Vertical Walls**

1. Remove nails and pry flashing [4] away from wall and sheathing.

2. Using putty knife and stiff brush, remove roofing cement from wall and sheathing.

▶ **Repair Wooden Surfaces**

This procedure shows how to repair sheathing [3] and other wood boards [1,2,5] which are used to support and fasten roofing materials.

Always repair or replace damaged sheathing or boards. The damaged sheathing or boards may cause roofing materials to loosen and be blown off by the wind or allow water to leak into the building.

If possible, replace and repair sheathing and boards with same type. Also, use the same size nails, same board widths, and the same spacing as the original sheathing.

1. Check hip and ridge boards [1,2] for decay, splits, or other damage. If boards are damaged, replace them.

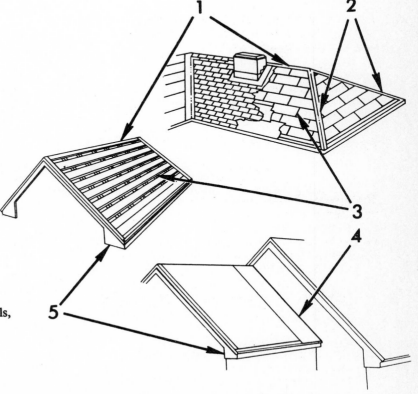

PREPARING THE ROOF

It is not necessary to remove a full sheet of plywood when only a small section is bad. You cut off and replace only the bad section.

Apply caulking where two pieces of plywood meet to prevent water from entering the plywood through the edges. Water will cause the plywood to deteriorate rapidly.

2. Check sheathing [1,4] and boards [2] at the gable edges. Replace sheathing or boards that are decayed, split, broken, warped, or damaged.

3. If your old roof had wooden or shake shingles and you plan to install them again, replace the cant strip [6]. Also, check false fascia boards [7]. Replace decayed, split, or warped boards.

4. Replace the bottom sheathing board [5] at the edge of all the eaves.

5. Check all other sheathing [3,4]. Replace sheathing boards that are decayed, split, broken, warped, or damaged.

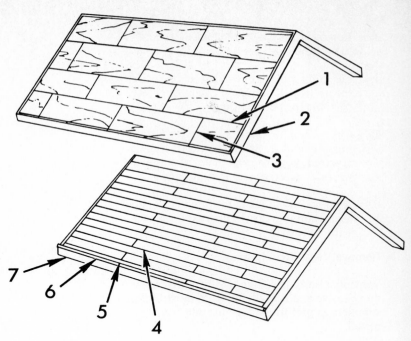

6. Cover knot holes in sheathing with a tin patch. Cut the patch 1 inch larger than the knot hole. Nail the patch to the sheathing with galvanized roofing nails.

▶ **How to Make a Chalk Line**

You will need to make chalk lines while installing roofing materials. Chalk lines will help you install materials in a straight line. Make a chalk line between marks using following procedures.

1. Install tacks on marks.

2. Tie one end of string to one of the tacks.

3. Pull string tight and tie other end of string to second tack.

4. Rub string with colored chalk.

5. Hold string tight between tacks and pull string slightly away from roof surface. Release string.

6. Chalk should mark straight line on roof surface. If you cannot see the chalk line on roof, repeat Steps 4 and 5 until you can see chalk line clearly.

7. Remove tacks and string.

▶ **Install Underlayment**

Underlayment should not be used for wooden or shake shingled roofs. Moisture trapped between the underlayment and shingles will cause the shingles to decay or be attacked by fungus.

Use 15 lb asphalt saturated felt roofing paper as underlayment. Roofing paper is sold in rolls 3 feet wide and 108 feet long. One roll will cover 324 square feet of roof.

CAUTION

Install composition roofing surface materials on dry surfaces only. If materials are installed on damp surfaces, wooden surfaces may decay or be attacked by fungi.

Drive nails straight in to avoid cutting roofing paper with nail heads.

Underlayment is installed in horizontal strips starting at the eaves and ending with an overlay of the ridge.

Align the underlayment with the edges of gables and eaves. Provide a 6 inch overlap [4] of hips [3], valley centerlines [1], and ridges [2].

Where underlayment forms horizontal seams [5], the top piece must overlap the lower piece by at least 2 inches. This overlap is called head lap.

If the strip of underlayment is not long enough to reach the opposite edge of the roof, provide a 4 inch overlap at side seams [6] where the two pieces meet. This overlap is called side lap.

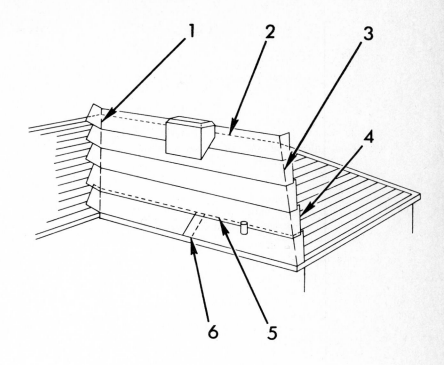

1. Place roll of underlayment paper on the roof. Unwind 4 feet of underlayment. Align edges of paper with the edges at the gable and eave of the roof. If one edge of the roof is a hip or valley, provide a 6 inch overlap at the centerline of the hip or valley.

2. Remove wrinkles. Temporarily nail top edge of underlayment to sheathing with roofing nails. Space nails 1 inch from edge and 24 inches apart.

At vent stack or chimney, cut outline [3] of vent stack or chimney in the strip of underlayment material.

3. Remove wrinkles and keep lower edge of underlayment aligned with the edge at the eaves or chalk line. Unwind material. Temporarily nail top edge until you reach the opposite edge of the roof or until the roll of material is completely unwound.

If roll of underlayment did not reach opposite edge of the roof, continue the strip with a new roll of underlayment in Step 4.

4. Unwind 4 feet of underlayment. Align lower edge with edge at eaves. Overlap [2] end of installed piece 4 inches. Repeat Steps 2 and 3.

5. If you have enough material to reach the opposite edge of the roof, cut material to align with the gable edge of the roof. If the edge of the roof is a hip or valley, cut material to overlap [1] the centerline of the hip or valley 6 inches.

6. Complete nailing underlayment strip to the sheathing. Space nails 1 inch from edges of strip and 8 inches apart. Avoid nailing in the spaces between sheathing boards.

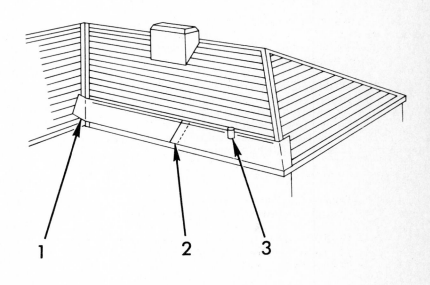

Install Underlayment

7. Mark ends [1,4] of reference line for head lap 12 inches from edge of roof and 2 inches below top edge of underlayment. Mark a chalk line [2] between marks. (See Page 14.)

8. Place roll of underlayment paper on the roof.

9. Unwind 4 feet of underlayment and align bottom edge with chalk line [2]. Align the end with the gable edge of the roof. If the edge is a hip or valley, overlap the center-line [5] of the hip or valley 6 inches. Repeat Steps 2 through 7.

10. Continue installing underlayment until the last strip is less than 28 inches [3] from the ridge.

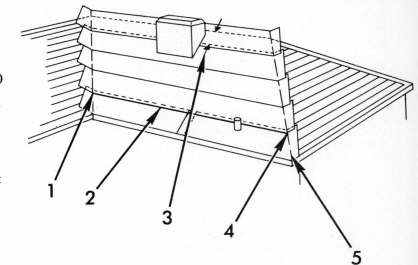

Use the following procedure to install the last strips to cover the ridge.

11. Place roll of underlayment paper on the ridge. Align top edge [2] of underlayment to overlay the ridge by at least 6 inches. Align the end with the gable edge of the roof. If the edge is a hip or valley overlap the centerline [1] by 6 inches.

12. Repeat Steps 2 through 5 for the last strips.

13. Use tin snips to cut and fit material to overlay intersecting ridges [3] at hips or valleys.

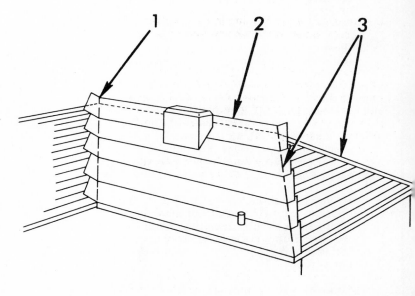

▶ **Install Metal Drip Edges**

Drip edges [1,2] should be installed along edges of gables and eaves.

Drip edges are normally made of aluminum, galvanized steel, or copper. Use nails made of the same materials as the drip edges to prevent corrosion. Drip edges for the edge at the eaves of the roof have a slight curve [4] to direct water away from fascia boards [3].

1. Measure the length of the edge of the roof. Cut drip edge to measured length.

2. Nail drip edge to roof with roofing nails. Space nails 1 inch from edge [5] no more than 10 inches apart.

CAUTION

If the places where two drip edge pieces meet are not sealed, the wood at the roof edges will decay quickly and will have to be replaced.

3. Use putty knife to apply asphalt roofing cement to places where two pieces of drip edges meet.

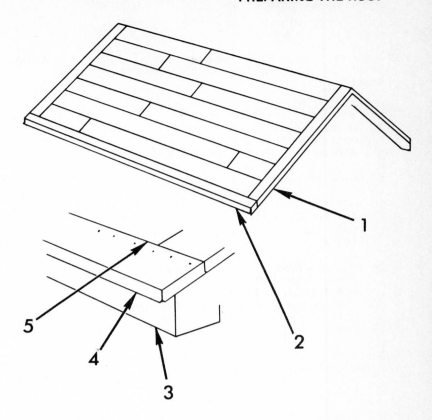

▶ **Install Eaves Flashings**

CAUTION

Do not install eaves flashing in cold weather. The flashing material will crack and lose its sealing properties.

Do not apply eaves flashing to a damp roof. The trapped moisture will cause wood support surfaces to decay and be attacked by fungus. To keep from cracking the flashing material, the roofing nails must be installed straight and with bottom of heads flush with flashing.

The eaves flashing strip must be installed with a 3/8 inch overhang on the drip edges [2,5] to keep out water.

Eaves flashing strips are made from 65 or 90 lb mineral-surfaced roll roofing material. Use 90 lb roofing material if available. It will last longer.

Do not overlap at centerlines [1] of valleys. The valleys will be sealed with other flashing. Flashing strips can be cut to meet at the centerlines or end 1/4 inch from the centerline.

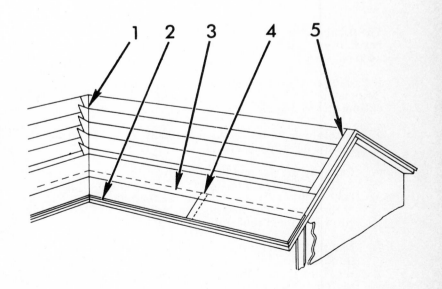

Where head laps [3] or side laps [4] are necessary, use a minimum of 6 inches overlap. Overlaps are to be cemented with **asphalt roofing lap cement** and nailed to sheathing. Avoid overlaps where possible.

PREPARING THE ROOF

Eaves flashing strips must be installed to cover the entire lower surface of the roof.

If you live in an area with moderate to heavy snowfall, install double thickness eaves flashings, Page 19.

Install Single Thickness Eaves Flashings

The 36 inch wide flashing strips are to be installed with a minimum of 6 inches head lap until the top of the eaves flashing is at least 12 inches [4] (24 inches if pitch of roof is 1/6 or less) past the inside wall line of the house. Where side laps are necessary use a minimum of 6 inches overlap.

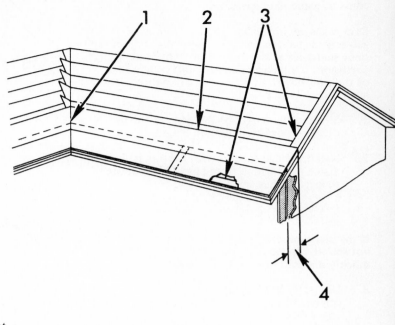

1. Measure and cut 36 inch wide eaves flashing strips [2] from 90 lb mineral-surfaced roll roofing.

2. Start at a lower corner of the roof and extend flashing strip 3/8 inch beyond drip edges [3]. If one edge of the roof is a valley or hip, align one corner of the flashing with the centerline [1]. The other corner should overlap the centerline.

3. Temporarily nail top edge of flashing strip with roofing nails. Start 2 feet from edge at gable or from centerlines of hips or valleys. Space nails 1 inch from top edge and 2 feet apart.

4. Using roofing knife and straightedge, cut end of flashing to match centerline.

CAUTION

The flashing strip [3] must be soft and easy to bend. If you crack the material, it will not keep out water.

If flashing cracks it will be necessary to replace it. You may be able to use the flashing strip by cutting off the damaged edge.

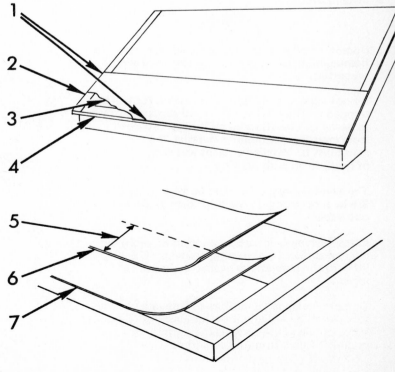

5. Carefully bend the 3/8 inch overhang against the drip edge [2,4].

6. Carefully lift side and lower edges [1] of flashing. Apply a 6 inch wide strip of roofing lap cement to the underside of the flashing at the edges. Press flashing onto drip edges [2,4] and roof surface.

7. Nail flashing to roof surface. Do not nail through drip edges. Start 1 inch from drip edges and space nails 4 inches apart. Apply roofing lap cement to nail heads.

Install Double Thickness Eaves Flashings

The 36 inch wide flashing strips [6,7], are to be installed with a minimum of 19 inches head lap [5] until the top of the eaves flashing is at least 12 inches (24 inches if pitch is 1/6 or less) past the inside wall line of the house. Where side laps are necessary, use a minimum of 6 inches overlap.

1. Cut 19 inch wide strips [3] from 90 lb mineral roll roofing.

The 19 inch wide flashing is to be installed with mineral (rough) surface down or toward roof surface.

2. Install 19 inch wide flashings using Steps 2 through 7 of the instructions on how to Install Single Thickness Eaves Flashings, Page 18.

3. Cut 36 inch wide flashing strips [1,2] from 90 lb mineral-surfaced roll roofing.

The 36 inch wide flashing [1,2] is to be installed with smooth surface toward 19 inch wide flashing [3] and roof.

4. Install 36 inch wide flashing using instructions on how to Install Single Thickness Eaves Flashing, Page 18.

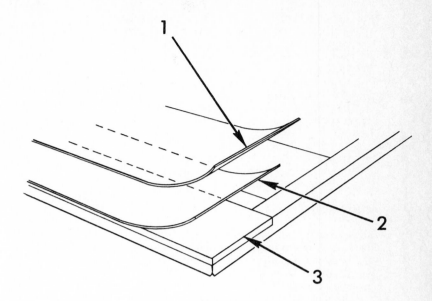

▶ **Install Chimney Flashings**

Chimney flashings are made from either corrosion resistant metal or roll roofing materials.

Corrosion resistant metal, properly applied, provides the most durable flashing. It is recommended that you use **only** metal flashing.

Flashing can be cut and shaped by a local sheet metal shop using the old pieces as patterns.

1. Cut and shape new flashing. Use old flashing pieces as patterns.

The top edges [2] of the cap flashing should be bent a minimum of 1-1/2 inches or a maximum of 3 inches. The bent edge will fit into the chimney mortar joints [1].

2. Check that mortar joints are deep enough to hold bent edge of cap flashing. If not, remove mortar to required depth using cold chisel and small sledge. Clean all mortar dust from joints and sheathing.

Lower flanges [3] of chimney flashings will be installed above shingles. Top and side flanges [4,5] will be covered by shingles.

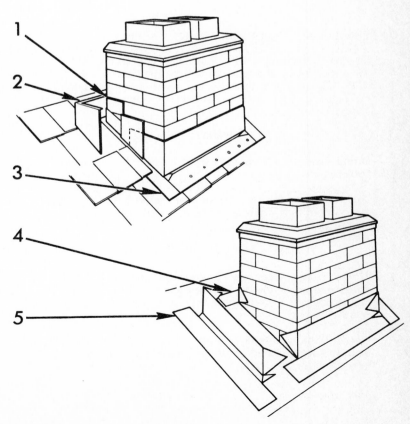

CAUTION

The nails used to nail the flashing to the sheathing must be made from the same material as the flashing pieces. Failure to use the same material will cause rapid corrosion of flashing.

PREPARING THE ROOF

Install Chimney Flashings

3. Install base flashing [2]. Nail flashing to sheathing. Apply asphalt roofing cement or caulking compound to all edges [1] of flashing and nail heads.

4. Apply a layer of clear butyl or aluminized compound to the back surfaces of the cap flashing [3]. Install cap flashing by pressing into place.

5. Apply caulking compound to all edges [4] of cap flashing. Fill the mortar joints into which the cap flashing is pressed with caulking compound.

▶ **Install Valley Flashings**

Valley flashing can be either open [6] or closed [5]. When flashing appears as a trough lying between the edges of the shingles, it is called open flashing. When flashing is covered by shingles, it is called closed flashing. Closed flashing is used to improve the appearance of the roof.

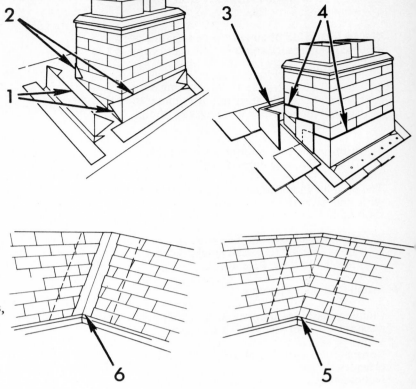

Install Composition Roofing Valley Flashings

Composition roofing valley flashing is constructed the same way for both open and closed type valley flashings. The color of the composition roll roofing should match the color of the shingles when constructing open type valley flashings.

WARNING

Do not heat cement directly over fire. Explosion or fire could occur.

Use small seats for yourself and for materials to avoid injury from falls when working on a roof with a pitch greater than 1/4.

CAUTION

Composition roll roofing flashing must be installed in mild weather. If temperature is too cool, the materials may crack and wrinkles may appear in flashing when weather warms.

Install flashing materials on dry surfaces only. If materials are installed on damp surfaces, wooden surfaces may decay or be attacked by fungi.

Drive nails straight in to avoid cutting roofing paper with nail heads.

Do not leave strips of roofing on lawn when warming in sun. Absorbed heat will burn lawn.

Valley flashing should be made in one continuous piece. If this is not possible, the higher piece must overlap the lower piece by at least 12 inches.

Roofing cement must be warm when used. An acceptable method of warming cement is to place can of cement into warm water.

If old flashing can be used as a pattern, go to Step 4 on next page.

1. Select a piece of scrap composition roofing material 18 inches wide and at least 30 inches long.

2. Center the 18 inch width of material on the valley with lower corners [4] extending beyond the eaves. Press material against roof surface to form contour of valley.

3. Using roofing knife, carefully cut vee outline of intersecting roofs [2]. Remove material.

4. Measure length of valley centerline [1]. Measure longest depth [3] of vee pattern. Add both measurements. Add 4 to 7 inches to allow for overhang of drip edges and cut and trim where valley meets the ridge of the roof. Record value on a piece of paper.

5. Using tape measure, straightedge, and roofing knife, cut an 18 inch wide strip [5] from roll of 90 lb composition roofing material to the length calculated in Step 4.

6. Using pattern [6], mark vee lines [7] in one end of 18 inch wide strip.

7. Using straightedge and roofing knife, cut along vee lines [7] and remove triangle piece [8].

CAUTION

The flashing strip must be soft and easy to bend to prevent cracking the material. Cracked material will not keep out water and must be replaced.

8. Place the strip of roofing material on the valley with mineral (rough) surface toward the roof.

9. Align strip on the centerline [1] of the valley. Extend edges of vee [2] 3/8 inch beyond drip edge.

10. Press flashing against the roof surfaces to form contour of valley. Bend edges of vee against drip edge.

11. Hold edges of vee [2] off roof surface and apply a 2 inch wide strip of roofing lap cement to the underside edges of the vee.

12. Align edges of vee. Carefully press cemented edges against roof and drip edges.

13. Using roofing knife, cut top edge [5] of flashing to fit contour of intersecting ridges [4].

14. Nail side edges [3] of flashing to sheathing with roofing nails 1 1/2 inches long. Space nails 1 inch from edge of material and 12 inches apart.

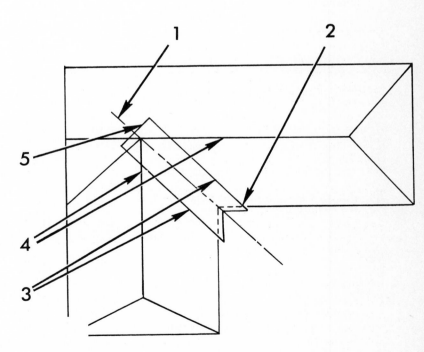

21

PREPARING THE ROOF

Install Composition Roofing Valley Flashings

15. Using tape measure, straightedge, and roofing knife, cut a 36 inch wide strip of 90 lb composition roofing material [1] 30 inches longer than the length of the valley centerline.

16. Place 18 inch wide [2] or 36 inch wide [3] pattern on mineral surface (rough) side of roofing material [1]. Mark lines of vee [4]. Remove pattern. Using straightedge and roofing knife, cut along lines of vee [4] and remove triangle piece [5].

17. Place the strip of roofing material [1] on the 18 inch wide strip with mineral surface up. Repeat Steps 9, 10, and 13 before continuing.

18. Remove 36 inch wide strip and place to one side on roof.

19. Apply 3 inch wide strip of roofing lap cement to all edges of the 18 inch under strip. Apply a 2 inch wide strip of roofing lap cement to the underside edges of the 36 inch wide vee [4].

20. Place 36 inch wide strip on 18 inch wide strip. Align bent edges of vee against drip edges. Align centerline of the 36 inch wide strip with the centerline of the valley. Remove wrinkles.

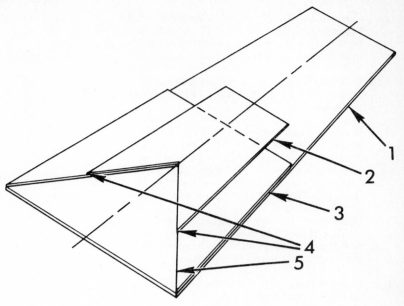

21. Carefully press cemented edges of 36 inch wide vee against drip edges. Press 36 inch wide strip firmly against cemented edges of 18 inch wide strip.

22. Nail flashing to sheathing. Space nails 1 inch from edges of material and 12 inches apart.

If installing an open type valley flashing, make chalk lines [3] to help install shingles the correct distances from the valley centerline [2].

23. Place a mark [1] on roof ridge line 3 inches from centerline [2] of valley.

24. Place a mark [4] on edge at eaves 4 inches from centerline [2] of valley.

25. Make a chalk line between the two marks [1,4]. See Page 14 on how to make a chalk line.

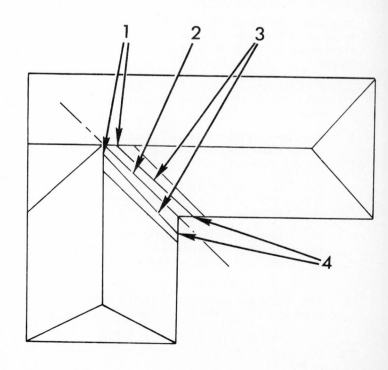

Install Metal Valley Flashings

CAUTION

Composition roll roofing must be installed in mild weather. If temperature is too cool, the materials may crack.

Install composition roofing surface materials on dry surfaces only. If materials are installed on damp surfaces, wooden surfaces may decay or be attacked by fungi.

Drive nails straight in to avoid cutting roofing paper with nail heads.

Do not leave strips of roofing on lawn when warming in sun. Absorbed heat will burn lawn.

Instructions for installing metal flashing are the same for open or closed valley flashing.

Purchase metal flashing from a sheet metal shop. Give old valley flashing to the sheet metal shop to use as a pattern. If they cannot use the old flashing as a pattern, you will have to provide the length of the valley and the pitch (see Page 7) of the roof surfaces [1,2] and [3,4] forming the valley.

When the pitch of the roof is 1/2 or more, the flashing must extend to at least 7 inches on

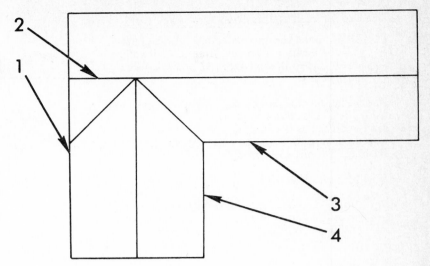

each side of the valley centerline. If the pitch is less than 1/2, the flashing must extend to at least 10 inches on each side of the valley centerline.

The metal flashing is installed over a 36 inch wide strip of 30 or 65 lb composition roll roofing.

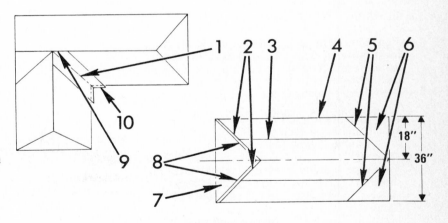

1. Measure the length of the valley center-line [1]. Add 30 inches to allow for cut of the vee [10].

2. Cut a 36 inch wide strip of 30 or 65 lb composition roll roofing to the length calculated.

3. Use the metal flashing [3] as a pattern. Mark lines [2,5] of vee on top and bottom ends of the 36 inch wide strip [4] of roll roofing.

4. Measure 3/8 inch from lines [2] and mark parallel lines [8] to allow for 3/8 inch overhang of drip edges.

5. Using straightedge and roofing knife, cut along lines [5,8] and remove triangle pieces [6,7].

6. Place the strip [4] of roofing material on the valley. Align the centerline of the material with the centerline [1] of the valley. Align the edges of the bottom vee [10] to overhang the edge of the drip edges 3/8 inches. Align the edges [5] of the top vee with the edges [9] of the intersecting ridges.

CAUTION

The flashing strip must be soft to prevent cracking the material. Cracked material will not keep out water and must be replaced.

7. Press roofing material against the roof surfaces to form contour of the valley. Carefully bend edges of vee [10] against drip edge.

8. Attach roofing material as described in Steps 11, 12 and 14 (Page 21) in the procedures for installing composition roofing valley flashing.

PREPARING THE ROOF

Install Metal Valley Flashings

9. Place metal flashing on valley. Align center-line of flashing with centerline [1] of valley. Push turned down edges [3] of vee against drip edges.

The metal flashing can be fastened to the sheathing using metal brackets [4] or nails made of the same material as the flashing. Brackets are preferred because they do not nail through the flashing. Do not nail through drip edges.

If using nails, go to Step 11.

10. Hold flashing to sheathing with brackets at sides [2] only. Place bracket over edge of flashing. Nail bracket to sheathing with roofing nails. Space brackets 8 inches apart.

11. If using nails, space nails 1/2 inch from edge of flashing and 8 inches apart. Nail at sides [2] only. Nail flashing to sheathing. Avoid nailing through the spaces between sheathing boards. Apply asphalt roofing cement on nail heads.

If installing open type valley, go to Page 22 (bottom) for instructions on how to make valley chalk lines.

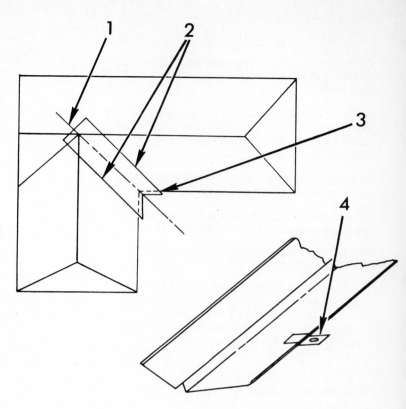

▶ Install Vent Pipe Flashings

Vent pipe flashing [2] can be purchased from most building material suppliers in a ready to install form. You will need to measure the outside diameter [4] of the pipe. Obtain flashing with flanges having at least the following lengths:

- 8 inches top [3] of vent
- 6 inches on each side [6] of vent
- 4 inches below [1] vent

Vent pipe flashing is installed when installing shingles. The flange below [1] vent is installed above shingles. The top [3] and side [6] flanges are to be covered by shingles. After installing shingles [7] up to a vent pipe, use instructions below to install vent flashing.

WARNING

Do not heat cement directly over fire. Explosion or fire could occur.

Roofing cement must be warm when used. An acceptable method of warming cement is to place can of cement in warm water.

1. Place flashing over vent stack. Align lower flange [8] with edges [9] of shingles.

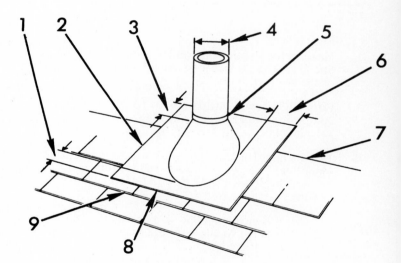

2. Nail flashing to sheathing with roofing nails of same materials as flashing. Space nails 1 inch from edge of flanges and 8 inches apart.

3. Fill space [5] between flashing and pipe with packing.

4. Apply asphalt roofing cement to space [5] between flashing and vent pipe and nail heads.

Install Flashings Between Roof and Vertical Walls

Flashings between roofs and vertical walls are made from 65 or 90 lb composition roofing material. If the vertical wall has a lap siding of boards, metal, or shingles, it is best to use flashing strips 12 inches long, bent to slide 4 inches up under the siding. If you can't push flashing under siding, install an 8 inch wide strip of composition roofing material along the vertical wall.

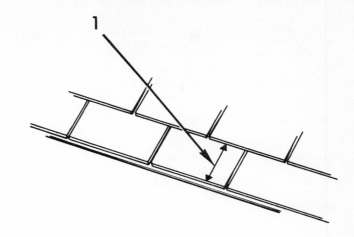

1.   Measure width of the roof along the vertical wall from the edge at the eaves to the ridge.

If installing an 8 inch wide flashing strip, go to Page 26, Step 12.

A 12 inch flashing strip is needed for each course of shingles to be installed. Make the width of the flashing strip 3 inches wider than the exposure [1] of the shingles. Use the following instructions to calculate the number of flashing strips you will need.

2.   Measure the exposure [1] of the shingles you plan to install. Divide the width of the roof by the exposure of the shingles.

For example,

173 inches width of roof
5 inches exposure of shingle
173/5 = 34.6 or 35 flashing strips will be needed.

3.   Cut flashing strips from sheet metal or 65 or 90 lb composition roofing material.

CAUTION

The flashing strip must be soft to prevent cracking the material. Cracked material will not keep out water and must be replaced.

4.   Align the edge [2] of a board 4 inches from the edge [1] of the flashing strip. Carefully bend the 4 inch end of the flashing strip up against the edge of the board.

5.   Repeat Step 4 until all the flashing strips are bent.

Flashing strips are installed overlapping the shingles. Therefore, you will have to install the flashing strips at the same time you install the shingles. The following instructions show how to install the flashing strips.

CAUTION

When installing wooden or shake shingles do not use asphalt roofing cement on side of flashing strips in contact with shingles. Wood will draw the oil out of the cement. The cement will cause the shingles to warp and split.

Roofing cement must be warm when used. An acceptable method of warming cement is to place can of cement in warm water.

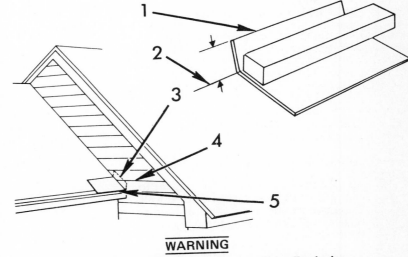

WARNING

Do not heat cement directly over fire. Explosion or fire could occur.

6.   Start at the eaves. Apply asphalt roofing cement to underside of flashing strip. Slide the 4 inch vertical end [3] of the flashing under the siding [4]. Align the horizontal edge [5] with the edge of the drip edge.

7.   Install starter and first course of shingles per instructions in next chapter (Page 27).

PREPARING THE ROOF

Install Flashings Between Roof and Vertical Walls

8. Apply asphalt roofing cement to underside of next flashing strip. Slide the flashing under the siding to overlap [2] the installed strip of flashing. Align the horizontal edge [1] 1 inch higher than the exposure of the shingle.

9. Install next course of shingles.

10. Repeat Steps 8 and 9 until you install the last course of shingles at the ridge.

11. Repeat Steps 8 and 9 to install flashing strip over last course of shingles at the ridge. Then install ridge shingles.

Steps 12 through 16 show how to install flashing to a roof when the vertical wall does not have lap siding.

12. Cut an 8 inch wide strip of flashing from 90 lb composition roofing material with a length equal to the width of the roof along the vertical wall.

13. Apply asphalt roofing cement to underside of flashing strip. Place flashing strip on roof. Align bottom edge [4] with the edge of the drip edge and push flashing strip against vertical wall [3].

14. Nail flashing to sheathing with roofing nails. Space nails 1 inch from edges and 10 inches apart.

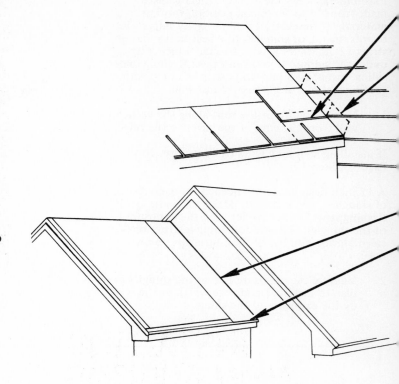

15. Apply a thick bead of roofing cement to edge [1] of flashing against vertical wall. Using putty knife, press edges of bead against vertical wall and flashing to bond cement to the flashing and wall.

16. Apply roofing cement to nail heads.

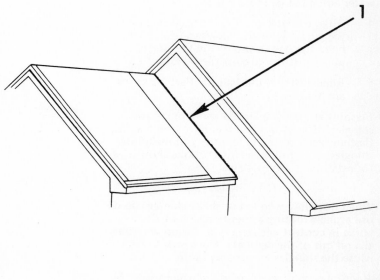

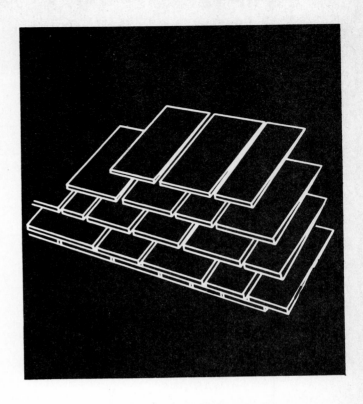

INSTALLING NEW ROOFING

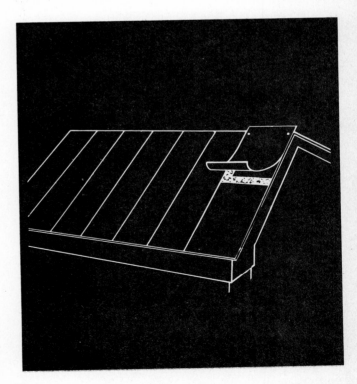

Asphalt strip form shingles are available in several patterns including three tab square butt strips [1], two tab hex strips [2], and three tab hex strips [3]. Procedures for all three are the same except:

● installing shingles as a starter course and

● starting subsequent courses.

Complete instructions are provided for installing the three tab square butt strips [1]. These instructions can also be used for two and three tab hex strips [2,3] with changes noted on Pages 35-36.

If you are **replacing** shingles, be sure to install an underlayment [4] per instructions on Pages 14-15.

Also, be sure to first install metal drip edges [6], chimney and vent flashings, and eaves flashing strips [5] per instructions on Pages 17-26.

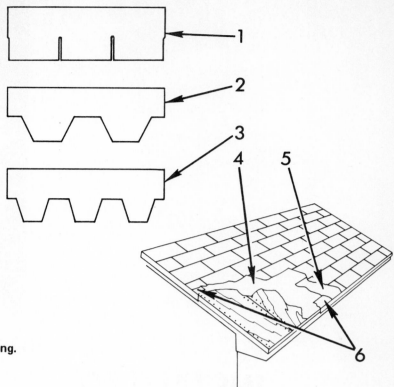

WARNING

Be sure to review the general safety rules before starting.

WARNING

Be sure to review the general safety rules before starting.

▶ **Tools and Supplies**

The following tools and supplies are needed to install asphalt shingles in strip form.

- Roofing knife [1] to cut and fit asphalt shingles.

- Hammer to nail asphalt shingles into place.

- Ladders and scaffolding [2] to get to the roof and to support you while working on lower portions of the roof.

- Chalk line [3] and chalk to help align shingle courses.

- Folding rule and steel tape [4] for measuring roofing surfacing material.

- A 2 inch wide paintbrush [5] for applying asphalt roofing lap cement.

- A putty knife [6] for applying asphalt roofing cement.

- Pre-formed hip and ridge asphalt shingles [7] to shingle hips and ridges.

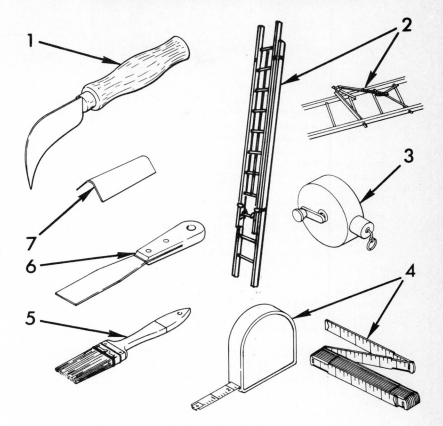

- 1-3/4 inch large headed galvanized roofing nails [1].

- Asphalt roofing cement, and asphalt roofing lap cement [2].

- 90 lb mineral surface roofing [3] (color must match shingles) to use as a starter strip. Starter strips are described on Page 30.

- A supply of asphalt shingle strips [4].

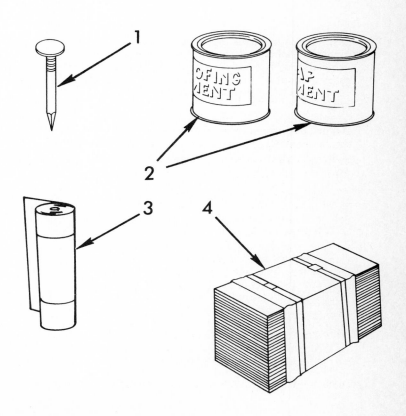

INSTALLING STRIP FORM ASPHALT SHINGLES

▶ **Install Composition Roll Roofing as Starter Course**

The starter course is installed below the first row or course [4] of shingles to provide a roofing edge [5] without indentations. Either **shingle strips** [2] or **composition roll roofing** [3] can be used as a starter course for any of the three different types of shingle strips. These materials are equally durable. Cost of roll roofing is slightly less than cost of shingle strips.

These instructions only show how to install **composition roll roofing** as a starter course. Instructions for installing **shingle strips** as a starter course are included in the installation instructions for the shingle strips of concern.

WARNING

Use small seats [1] for yourself and for materials to avoid injury from falls when working on a roof with a pitch greater than 1/4.

If shingle bundles are opened before you are ready to use them, the shingles may be blown about by the wind and cause injuries.

CAUTION

Composition roofing materials must be installed in mild weather. If temperature is too cool, materials may crack when installed.

Install composition roofing materials on dry surfaces only. If materials are installed on damp surfaces, wooden surfaces may decay or be attacked by fungi.

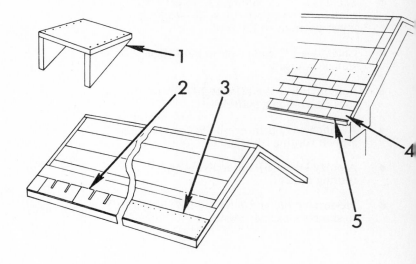

If starter course ends in a valley, measure length [6] of starter strip needed to reach from gable edge [7] to valley chalk line [5]. Be sure measurement of length [6] is made 12 inches [10] from eaves edge of roof to account for valley angle.

If starter course ends at a vertical wall or a hip, measure length [3] from gable edge to vertical wall or length [4] from gable edge to hip or wooden strip at hip.

1. Measure length [2] of starter course.

2. Unwind 90 lb mineral-surfaced roll roofing. Using roofing knife, cut starter course 12 inches wide and 3/4 inch longer than length of roof. If starter course ends at a valley chalk line [5], vertical wall or hip, cut starter course only 3/8 inch longer than length measured in Step 1.

3. Place starter course [9] on roof with mineral coated surface facing downward. Allow ends of course to extend 3/8 inch beyond gable edges [1] and eaves edge [8] of roof.

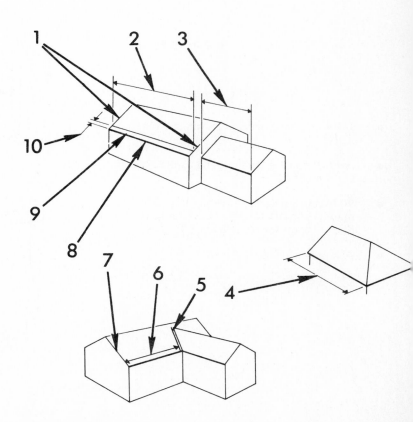

Roofing cement must be warm when used. An acceptable method of warming cement is to place can of cement in warm water.

WARNING

Do not heat roofing cement directly over fire. Explosion or fire could result.

4. If course ends at a valley chalk line [3] or a vertical wall [1], apply a 6 to 8 inch wide strip of asphalt cement [2] to flashing next to valley chalk line or wall.

5. Press end of starter course into asphalt cement.

Use 1-3/4 inch galvanized roofing nails to install asphalt shingles. Nails should penetrate 3/4 inch into wood. If nails show through sheathing at eaves overhang, use shorter nails in this area only.

CAUTION

Drive nails straight in to avoid cutting roofing paper with nail heads.

6. Nail starter course [6] in place with nails [4]. Space nails 8 inches apart and 1 inch in from top [7] and sides [5] of strip.

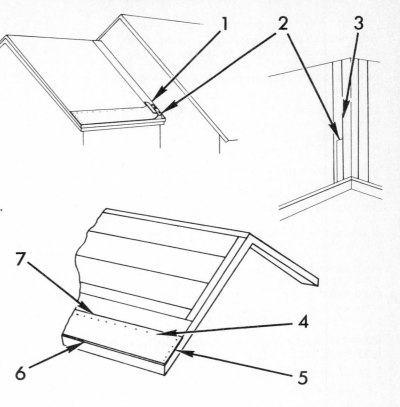

▶ **Install Three Tab Square Butt Strip Shingles**

If you have already installed composition roll roofing as starter course, go to Step 9, Install First Course.

<u>Install Shingles as Starter Course</u>

1. Start the course with a partial shingle strip [4]. Cut partial shingle strip so that the joint between it and next shingle will be completely covered by a tab on the first shingle strip of the first course.

2. Place partial shingle strip [4] on lower corner of roof with tab [1] or tabs pointing toward ridge of roof and mineral-coated surface down. Extend strip 3/8 inch beyond gable edge [2] and eaves edge [3].

Use nails that are not long enough to go through the sheathing at the eaves [6].

3. Nail strip [4] to sheathing with three nails [5]. Be sure the nails pierce metal drip edges [8].

4. Continue starter course with full sized shingle strips [7], using four nails per strip. The nailing pattern should be such that all nails [9] will be covered by the tabs [10] on the first course of shingles.

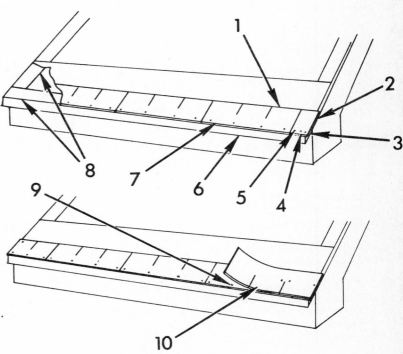

Read the next few steps before installing last two shingle strips.

INSTALLING STRIP FORM ASPHALT SHINGLES

Install Shingles as Starter Course

Both next to last shingle strip [1] and last shingle strip [2] in all rows must be at least 6 inches wide at butt line [4]. If necessary adjust widths of both shingle strips to provide 6-inch widths at butt line.

Shingles should **not** be installed in valleys. Chalk lines made during preparation are the borders for the valley. The shingles should be installed to the chalk lines and not into the valley.

5. Cut last shingle strip [2] to fit along valley chalk line [3], hip, or vertical wall. If course ends at a gable, extend last shingle strip 3/8 inch beyond gable molding.

If course ends at a gable or hip, go to Step 8. If not, continue.

Asphalt roofing cement must be warm when used. An acceptable method of warming cement is to place can of cement in warm water.

WARNING

Do not heat asphalt roofing cement directly over fire. Explosion or fire could result.

6. If course ends at a valley chalk line [3] or a vertical wall [5], apply a 6 to 8 inch wide strip of asphalt roofing cement [6] to flashing next to chalk line or wall.

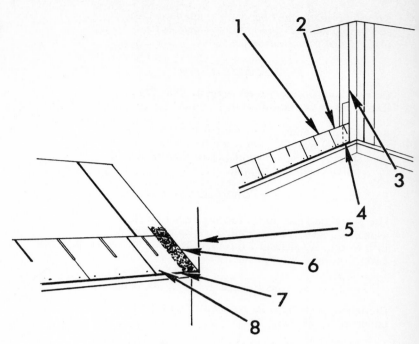

7. Press shingle strip [7] into asphalt roofing cement [6].

8. Nail shingle strip to sheathing with two galvanized roofing nails [8].

Install First Course

9. Place a whole strip [1] of shingles at a gable corner [3] with mineral surface up and tabs [2] down. Align butt end [5] and side [4] of shingle strip with starter course shingle strip underneath.

If shingle strips were used for starter course, go to Step 11. If composition roll roofing was used for starter course, continue.

Large headed roofing nails [7] for starter course must be covered by tabs [6] on first course of shingles.

Be careful to drive nails straight in so that shingle surfaces are not cut or dented.

10. Lift tabs [6] on first course shingle and nail starter course. Nails [7] for starter course should be 8 inches apart at lower edge of starter course and go through metal drip edges [8] into sheathing.

11. Lift first shingle strip up and place daubs of cement over the nails [7] in the starter course. Press shingle strip onto daubs of cement.

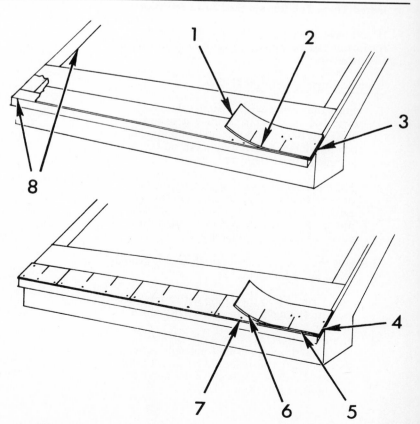

12. Nail shingle strip in place with six galvanized roofing nails. Hammer nails in on a line just above the ends of the shingle slots [1]. Two pairs of nails [2] should be near the shingle slots and the other nails [3] should be 1 inch in from the shingle strip edges.

13. Continue to install the first row of shingle strips to the other end of the roof. Read next few steps before installing last two shingle strips.

Both next to last shingle strip [6] and last shingle strip [5] in all rows must be at least 6 inches wide at butt line [7]. If necessary adjust widths of both shingle strips to provide 6 inch widths at butt line.

14. Cut the last shingle strip to fit end of last shingle strip of starter course.

If last shingle strip ends at a gable [9] or hip [8], nail it in place and go to Step 17. If not continue.

15. Apply a 6 to 8 inch wide coating of asphalt cement [4] to starter course next to chalk line or vertical wall.

16. Press shingle strip into asphalt cement and nail in place.

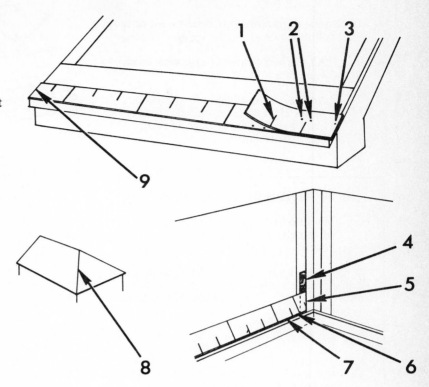

Install Second and Succeeding Shingle Courses

17. Place first shingle strip of second course [1] so that notches [2] in the second row are aligned with the center of the tabs [4] in the first row. Using roofing knife, cut off extra portion of shingle extending beyond gable edge [8]. Extend strip to 3/8 inch beyond gable edge.

18. Place second row of shingles so that entire tab [4] on first course of shingles [3] is exposed.

19. Nail each shingle strip in place with six nails [9]. Locate nails in a line 5-5/8 inches above butt end of strip. Nails should be 1 inch in from ends of strip and 1-1/2 inches on each side of slots.

20. Install third [5] course in same manner as first two courses. Notches [6] for third course should be aligned with notches [7] in first course.

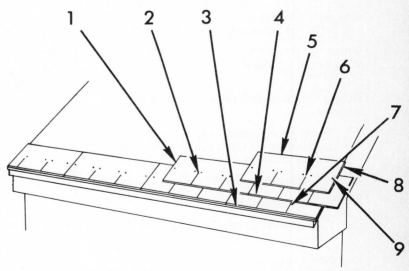

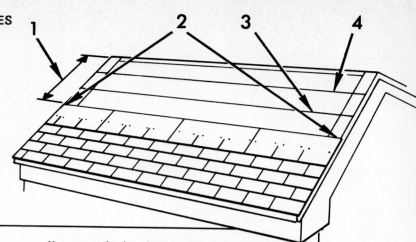

21. Continue with remaining courses but note the following:

    a. Align every fourth course with chalk line (Page 14).

    b. Adjust course alignment when top edge [2] of installed shingles is approximately 6 feet from ridge of roof. Use instructions below.

HOW TO ADJUST COURSE ALIGNMENT

a. Measure distance [1] from top edge [2] of shingles to ridge at each end of shingle course.

    If distance [1] at each end differs by less than 1 inch, make a chalk line (Page 14) 2 feet above top edge [2] of shingles. Go to Step d. If not continue.

b. Divide difference in distance [1] measured by 3. Add result to 2 feet.

c. On end with longest distance [1], make a mark above top edge [2] of shingles at distance calculated in Step b. On opposite end, make a mark 2 feet above top edge [2] of shingles. Make a chalk line (Page 14) between marks.

d. Make second chalk line halfway between first chalk line [3] and ridge of roof.

e. Use chalk lines to align remaining courses of shingles.

Use instructions on below for installing shingles around chimneys or vents.

Use instructions on Page 37 for installing shingles on hips and ridges.

HOW TO INSTALL SHINGLES AROUND CHIMNEYS AND VENTS

Flashings at chimneys and vent pipes are installed when shingles are installed.

Lower flanges [2] of flashings at chimneys and vent pipes are installed above shingles. Top and side flanges of flashing are covered by shingles [1].

Where shingles meet chimneys and vents, shingles [3] are cut to fit around the chimney or vent.

Do not nail through flashings unless absolutely necessary.

a. Where shingle course meets lower edge of chimney or vent, cut shingles [4] to fit around chimney or vent.

b. Nail shingles to sheathing.

c. Install flashing, Pages 19 and 24.

d. Continue shingling. Cut shingles [1] to fit around chimney or vent above flashing.

e. Apply a 6 inch wide strip [5] of asphalt roofing cement to flashing next to chimney or vent and press shingle into asphalt roofing cement.

f. Nail shingles to sheathing. If nails go through flashing apply daubs of asphalt roofing cement on heads of nails.

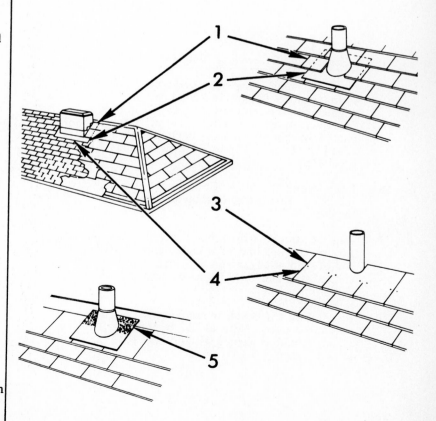

▶ **Install Three Tab Hex Strip Shingles**

These procedures only show how to install three tab hex strip shingles as a starter course and how to start each course. For detailed instructions, use the procedure for installing three tab square butt strip shingles (Page 31).

Install Three Tab Hex Shingle Strips as a Starter Course

1. Cut 6 inches [3] from width of a shingle strip.

2. Start starter course for three tab hex strip shingles with hex strip shortened by 6 inches. Place shingle strip [6] with mineral surface facing downward and tabs [1] pointed toward roof ridge line [2]. Allow shingle strip to extend 3/8 inch beyond gable edge [4] and eaves edge [5].

The starter course should be nailed in place with nails that are not long enough to go through the sheathing at the eaves.

3. Nail strip [6] in place with four nails. Locate nails [7] at lower edge of strip to go through metal drip edges [8] and to fall below tabs on first shingle course.

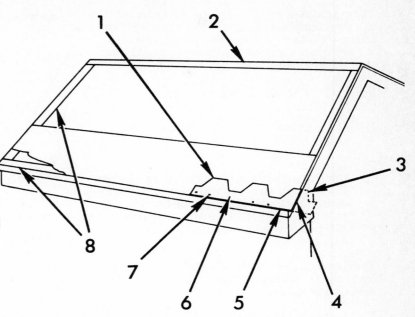

Start Shingle Courses

4. Start first course with a full shingle strip [5].

5. Start second course with a shingle strip shortened by 6 inches [4].

6. Start third course [1] the same as the first.

7. Start fourth course [2] the same as the second.

8. Attach each shingle with four roofing nails [3].

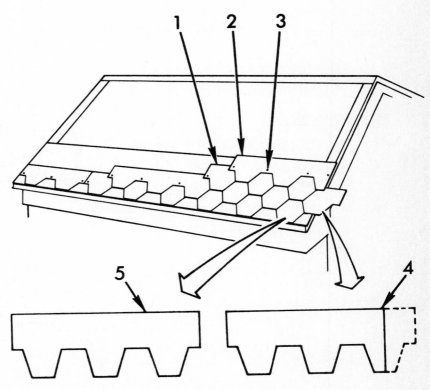

INSTALLING STRIP FORM ASPHALT SHINGLES

▶ **Install Two Tab Hex Strip Shingles**

These procedures only show how to install two tab hex strip shingles as a starter course and how to start each course. For detailed instructions, use the procedure for installing three tab square butt strip shingles (Page 31).

Install Two Tab Hex Shingle Strips as a
Starter Course

1. Cut 9 inches [4] from width of a shingle strip.

2. Start starter course for two tab hex strip shingles with hex strip shortened by 9 inches. Place shingle strip [8] with mineral surface facing down and tabs [3] pointed toward roof ridge line [2]. Extend shingle strip 3/8 inch beyond gable edge [5] and eaves edge [6].

The starter course should be nailed in place with nails that are not long enough to go through the sheathing at the eaves.

3. Nail strip [8] in place with galvanized roofing nails. Locate nails [7] at lower edge of strip to go through metal drip edges [1] and to fall below tabs on first shingle course.

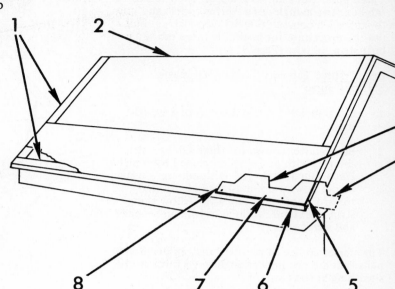

Start Shingle Courses

4. Start first course with a full shingle strip [5].

5. Start second course with a shingle strip shortened by 9 inches [4].

6. Start third course [1] the same as the first.

7. Start fourth course [2] the same as the second.

8. Attach each shingle with four roofing nails [3].

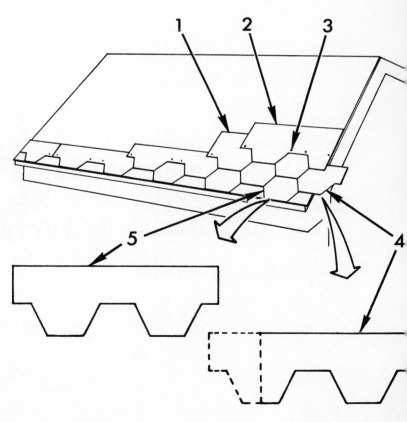

▶ **Finish Hips and Ridges**

Install 9 x 12 inch overlapping strips [3] of mineral-surfaced roll roofing on hips and ridges. The regular pattern is called a Boston hip and ridge.

If using commercially prepared hip and ridge shingles, go to Step 3.

1. Using roofing knife, cut 9 x 12 inch strips [1] of 90 lb mineral surfaced roll roofing. Select color suitable for use with shingle strip color.

2. Bend strips to fit over hips or ridges along 12 inch long centerline [2].

3. Cut first shingle [4] to fit at a lower end of hip. Allow shingle to extend 3/8 inch beyond edges [5].

4. Apply thin layer of asphalt cement to entire underside of first strip. Limit use of cement, especially in area of roofing nails, to prevent excess from running out over adjacent shingles.

5. Press shingle [4] onto hip with cement coated side down.

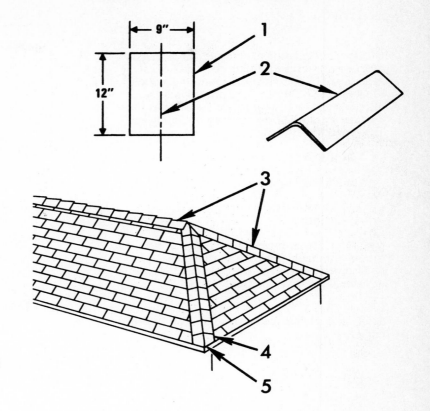

6. Nail shingle to hip with two galvanized 1-1/2 inch roofing nails [3] 5-1/2 inches [5] from upper end of shingle and 1 inch [4] in from each side. Upper end [2] will be covered by next shingle.

7. Proceed up hips and along ridges after reading a, b, c, and d below.

   a. Allow each additional strip to overlap preceding strip [6] by 6 inches [1].

   b. Apply thin layer of asphalt roofing cement to underside of each strip and press in place.

   c. Nail each shingle in place with two 1-1/2 inch galvanized roofing nails 5-1/2 inches from upper end of shingle and 1 inch in from each side.

   d. Cut last ridge shingle [7] to fit.

8. Apply daubs of roofing cement to exposed nail heads [8] on last ridge shingle [7].

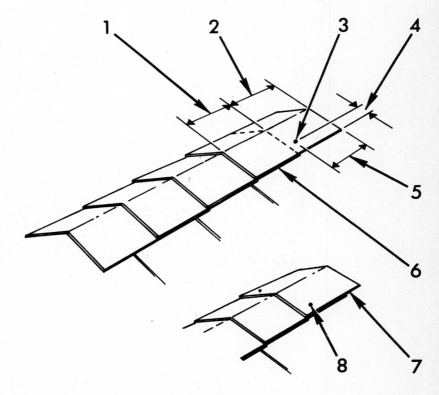

37

Giant individual asphalt shingles can be installed in several patterns including giant individual American [1], Dutch lap [2], and individual hexagonal [3]. Most of the procedures for installing all three patterns are the same as those used for installing strip form asphalt shingles. The principle differences in installation are that:

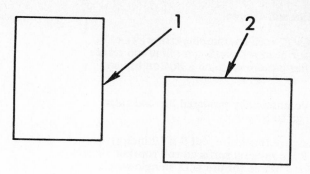

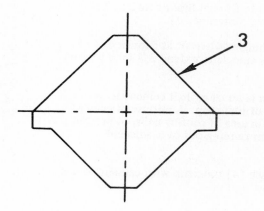

- giant individual American [1] and Dutch lap [2] patterns use starter courses and the individual hexagonal [3] pattern does not.

- subsequent shingle courses are started differently.

Complete instructions are provided for installing the giant individual American shingle pattern. For instructions on the Dutch lap and individual hexagonal patterns, see Contents below.

See Page 9 for index to instructions on how to prepare the roof.

WARNING

Be sure to review the general safety rules before starting.

▶ Tools and Supplies

The tools and supplies used for installing individual asphalt shingles are similar to those used for installing strip form asphalt shingles, Page 29. However, the following items are not needed:

a.   90 lb mineral surface roll roofing
b.   Asphalt roofing lap cement
c.   Two inch wide paintbrush

▶ General Instructions

WARNING

Use small seats [1] for yourself and for materials to avoid injury from falls when working on a roof with a pitch greater than 1/4.

If shingle bundles [2] are opened before you are ready to use them, the shingles may be blown about by the wind and cause injuries.

CAUTION

Individual asphalt shingles must be installed in mild weather. If temperature is too cool, shingles may crack when installed.

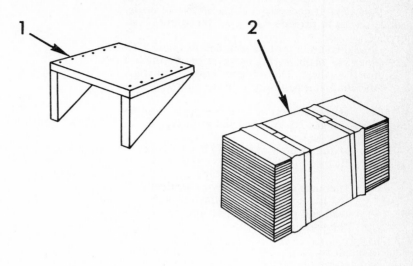

Install individual asphalt shingles on dry surfaces only. If shingles are installed on damp surfaces, wooden surfaces may decay or be attacked by fungi.

▶ Install Giant Individual American Shingles

Install Starter Course

1.   Place first shingle [3] in starter course with its long side [2] along eaves [7] and mineral-coated surface down. Allow shingle to extend 3/8 inch beyond gable edge [4] and eaves edge [7].

CAUTION

Drive nails straight in to avoid cutting shingle surfaces with nail heads.

Use 1-3/4 inch galvanized roofing nails to install asphalt shingles. Nails should penetrate 3/4 inch into wood. If nails show through sheathing at eaves overhang, use shorter nails in this area only. The nailing pattern should be such that all nails will be covered by shingles in the first course of shingles.

2.   Nail shingle to sheathing [1] with three galvanized roofing nails [5]. Be sure the nails [5] pierce metal drip edge [9].

3.   Continue starter course [6] with full sized shingles laid horizontally. Place each shingle against shingle next to it [8] with no gap between shingles. Read next few steps before installing last two shingles.

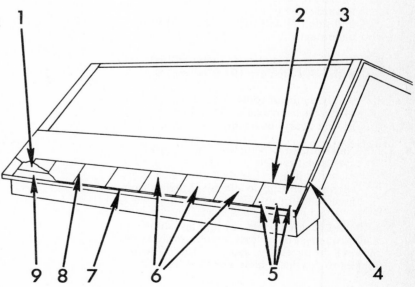

INSTALLING INDIVIDUAL ASPHALT SHINGLES

Both next to last shingle [8] and last shingle [6] in all rows must be at least 6 inches wide at butt line [7]. If necessary, adjust widths of both shingles to provide 6 inch widths at butt line.

Shingles should not be installed in valleys. Chalk lines [4] made during preparation are the borders for the valley. The shingles should be installed to the chalk lines and not into the valley.

4. **If course ends at a gable edge**, extend last shingle 3/8 inch beyond molding.

    If course ends at a hip [1], cut last shingle to fit hip.

    If course ends at a valley or vertical wall [2], cut last shingle to fit valley chalk line [4] or wall and perform Steps a and b after reading the warning.

Asphalt roofing cement must be warm when used. An acceptable method of warming cement is to place can of cement in warm water.

WARNING

Do not heat asphalt roofing cement directly over fire. Explosion or fire could occur.

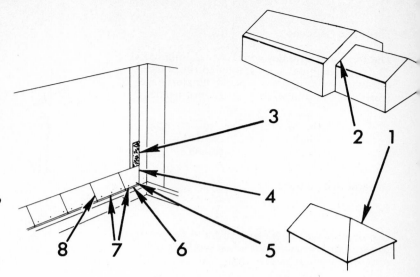

a. Apply a 6 to 8 inch wide strip of asphalt roofing cement [3] to flashing next to chalk line or vertical wall.

b. Press shingle [6] into asphalt roofing cement [3].

5. Nail shingle to sheathing with two roofing nails [5].

Install First Course

6. Place first shingle [2] at a gable corner with mineral coated surface facing upwards. Shingle long dimension must run from eaves toward ridge of roof. Align butt end [8] and side [7] with starter course shingle underneath.

7. Place second shingle [1] next to first shingle with a 3/4 inch gap [9] between shingles.

8. Apply daubs of roofing cement to heads of **starter** course nails [11]. Press shingles in **first** course into daubs of cement.

9. Nail shingles in place with two 1-3/4 inch galvanized roofing nails [10] with 3/8 inch diameter heads. Locate nails 1 inch in from each side of shingle and 5-1/2 inches from lower edge of shingle.

Both next to last shingle [6] and last shingle [4] in all rows must be at least 6 inches wide at butt lines [5]. If necessary, adjust widths of both shingles to provide 6 inch widths at butt line.

10. Install all but the last shingle.

11. **If course ends at a gable or hip,** cut last shingle to fit last shingle in starter course underneath.

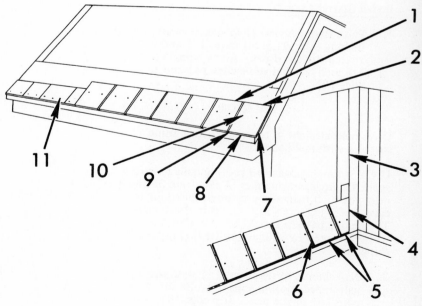

If course ends at a valley or vertical wall, cut last shingle to fit valley chalk line [3] or vertical wall and perform Steps a and b on next page.

a. Apply a 6 to 8 inch wide strip [2] of asphalt roofing cement to starter course [10] next to chalk line [1] or vertical wall [3].

b. Press last shingle in first course into asphalt roofing cement.

12. Nail shingle in place.

Install Second Course

Provide 5 inch exposure [9] for first course of shingles.

13. Set 5 inch exposure [4] on shingling hatchet with adjustable weather exposure gauge [5].

14. Use 6 inch wide shingle for first shingle [7]. Install first shingle [7] at gable edge [6] with side aligned with shingle in first course. Using weather exposure gauge [5], align both sides of butt end of shingle [8] for 5 inch exposure [9].

15. Nail shingle in place with two nails.

16. Install full size shingles for remainder of second course.

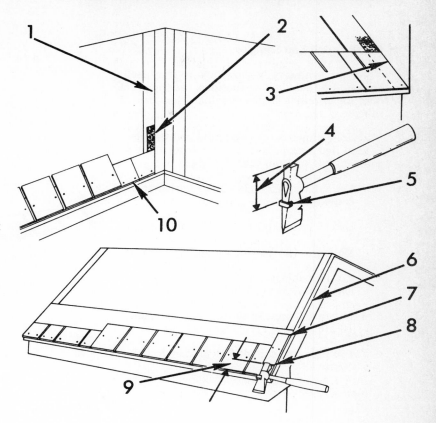

Install Third and Succeeding Courses

17. Continue with remaining courses but note the following:

a. Use a full size shingle [2] as first shingle in third course.

b. Use a 6 inch wide shingle [3] as first shingle in fourth course.

c. Repeat pattern as shingling continues.

d. Make a chalk line [1] after every fourth course to check that courses are straight (Page 14).

e. When within 6 feet of roof ridge, adjust course alignment, using instructions on Page 34.

Use instructions on Page 34 for installing shingles around chimneys or vent pipes.

Use instructions on Page 37 for installing shingles on hips and ridges.

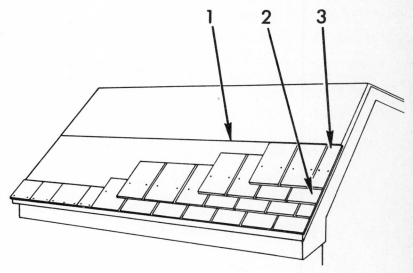

INSTALLING INDIVIDUAL ASPHALT SHINGLES

▶ Install Dutch Lap Shingles

These procedures only show how to start each course. For detailed instructions, use the procedure for installing giant individual American shingles (Page 39).

Place long dimension [6] of full sized shingles used in first, second, etc. courses from gable to gable instead of from eaves to ridge.

1. Use full sized shingle [5] to start first course.

2. Use 10 inch exposure [7] for all shingles.

3. Make gap [8] between shingles 7/8 inch.

4. Cut first shingle [3] in second course to length of 4-3/4 inches [4].

5. Cut first shingle in third course to length of 10-3/8 inches [1].

6. Use full sized shingle [2] to start fourth course.

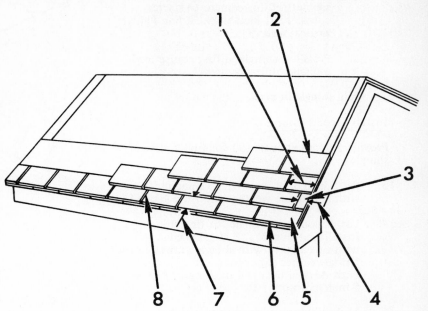

▶ Install Individual Hex Shingles

These procedures only show how to start each course. Individual hex shingles are installed without a starter course. For detailed instructions, use the procedure for installing giant individual American shingles (Page 39).

If roofing in windy location, add rake starter strips [4] of roll roofing at all gables [2]. Rake starter strip is mounted to 1 x 6 wood edging strip [3] at gables. If rake starter strip is not used, go to Step 7.

1. Remove metal drip edges at gables (Page 12).

2. Trim sheathing at gable [2] of roof back from edges a distance of 5-5/8 inches.

3. Fasten 1 x 6 wood edging strip [3] to rafters with galvanized 6 or 8 penny common nails.

4. Install metal drip edges (Page 17).

5. Cut 6 inch wide rake starter strips [4] of 60 lb roll roofing to fit from ridges [1] to eaves [6].

6. Nail rake starter strips [4] to 1 x 6 wood edging strip [3] with 1-1/2 inch galvanized roofing nails [5]. Space nails 8 inches apart and 1 inch in from both edges of edging strip.

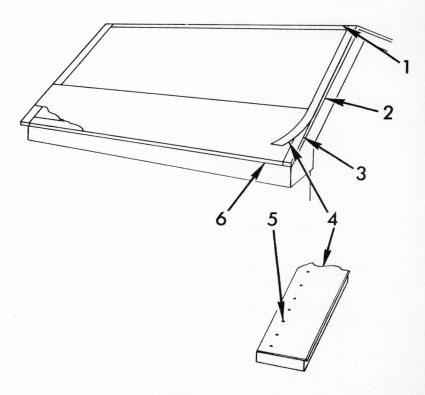

Only the top halves [8] of shingles are used in the first course. The first course [4] is started with the top right quarter [6] of a shingle.

7. Cut all shingles for first course across horizontal centerline [9]. Also, cut end shingle along its vertical centerline [7].

8. Align edges of quarter shingle [6] to overlap both gable and eaves edge of roof by 3/8 inch.

Roofing cement must be warm when used. An acceptable method of warming cement is to place can of cement in warm water.

<u>WARNING</u>

Do not heat roofing cement directly over fire. Explosion or fire could result.

9. Apply asphalt roofing cement to underside of shingle.

10. Press shingle onto eaves flashing strip [1].

Hex shingles are fastened to sheathing with two 1-3/4 inch galvanized roofing nails [2] per shingle. Nails are spaced 1 inch from edges of shingle on shingle horizontal centerline (1 inch higher for first course).

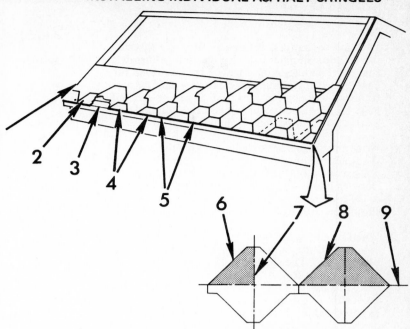

11. Nail shingle in place. Locate nails to pass through metal drip edge [3] and to be hidden by shingles [5] in next higher course.

12. Repeat Steps 9, 10, and 11 to install other shingles in first course.

Use full size shingles for second course.

13. Install second course [3]. Align lower edge of shingles to overlap edge of drip edge [2] by 3/8 inch. Second course [3] shingles should overlap first course shingles on both sides [5].

14. Apply daub [4] of asphalt roofing cement under tab of each shingle and press shingle into place.

15. Nail shingles in place with two 1-3/4 inch galvanized roofing nails [1] per shingle.

Third course is started with a shingle [7] cut in half along its vertical centerline. Fourth course is started with a full size shingle [6].

16. Repeat pattern of starting courses as shingling continues. Continue shingling.

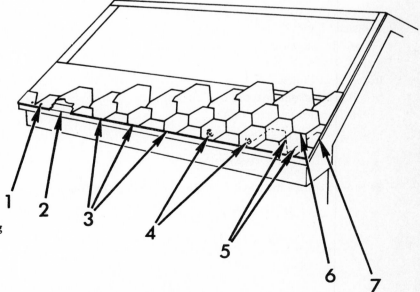

With a few changes, the instructions for install-ing wooden shingles can also be used to install shakes. The necessary changes are described on Page 50. If installing shakes, review the instruc-tions for wooden shingles first. Then go to Page 50 for the changes but use the detailed instructions for wooden shingles.

Wooden shingles are usually sold by the square. A square of shingles covers 100 square feet and consists of 1,000 shingles. The width [4] of shingles in any square will range from 4 inches to 14 inches. Shingles more than 8 inches wide should be split and nailed as two shingles.

When replacing shingles, use the same length [2] shingle and the same exposure [1] used on your old roofing. The sheathing [3] was located for the old exposure.

Exposure [1] is the distance each shingle is exposed below the butt (or thick) ends of the next course of shingles. Acceptable shingle exposures are given in the following table.

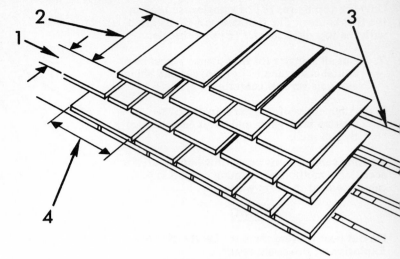

Shingle Length	*Standard Exposure	**Exposure for Roofs with Low Pitch
16 inches	5 inches	3-3/4 inches
18 inches	5-1/2 inches	4-1/4 inches
24 inches	7-1/2 inches	5-3/4 inches

*For pitch of 1/5 or greater
**For pitch of less than 1/5

(See Page 7 for definition of pitch.)

WARNING

Be sure to review the general safety rules before starting.

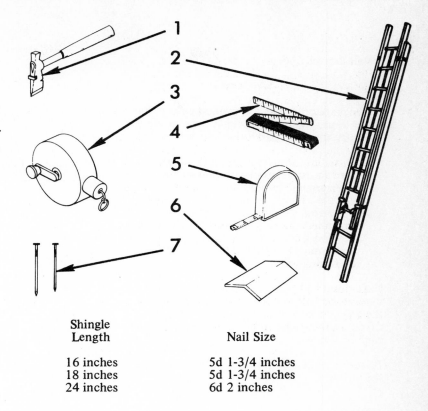

▶ Tools and Supplies

The following tools and supplies are needed to install wooden shingles:

- Shingling hatchet [1] with adjustable weather exposure gauge to cut and fit wooden shingles.

- Ladders and scaffolding [2] to get to the roof and to support you while working on lower portions of the roof.

- Chalk line [3] and chalk to help align shingle courses.

- Folding rule [4] or steel tape [5] for measuring alignment of shingle courses.

- A supply of wooden shingles.

- Precut hip and ridge wooden shingles [6].

- Shingling nails [7]. Use needle pointed nails to avoid splitting shingles. Nails should be rust resistant. The size nails to use depends upon the shingle length.

Shingle Length	Nail Size
16 inches	5d 1-3/4 inches
18 inches	5d 1-3/4 inches
24 inches	6d 2 inches

▶ General Instructions

WARNING

Use small seats [1] when working on a roof with a pitch greater than 1/4. The seats will help keep you and the materials from falling off the roof.

CAUTION

Do not use underlayment when shingles are replaced. An underlayment will reduce air circulation and moisture will collect under the underlayment. Such moisture can cause the wooden surface to decay or be attacked by fungi. Be sure to install eaves flashing. Instructions for installing eaves flashing is found on Page 17.

To prevent damage to new shingles, do not carry heavy shingle bundles across newly shingled roof.

If installing shakes, review instructions on Page 50 before continuing.

The starter row or course [3] is installed **below** the first course [2] of shingles to provide a roofing edge [4] without indentations. The starter course is made of standard wooden shingles.

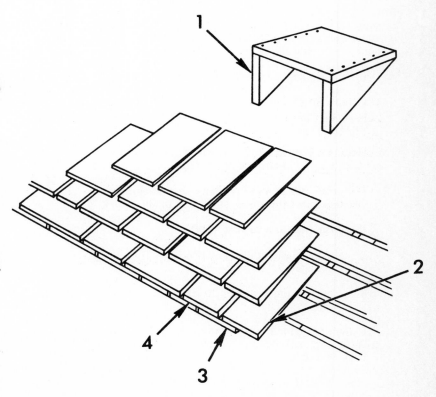

INSTALLING WOODEN SHINGLES

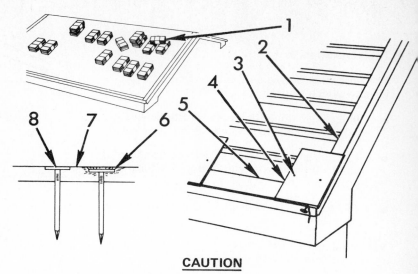

▶ **Install Starter Course**

WARNING

If shingle bundles [1] are opened before you are ready to use them, the shingles may be blown about by the wind and cause injuries.

1. Distribute shingle bundles [1] for one side of roof to different places on roof. Do not open shingle bundles until ready to use them.

2. Place first shingle [4] at gable edge with side extended 1/2 to 3/4 inch (1 inch for shakes) beyond gable molding [2] and butt (or thick) end extended 1-1/2 inches beyond the sheathing [5].

Nails should be 1 to 1-1/2 inches above the exposure line and 3/4 inch (1 inch for shakes) from the sides of each shingle. Nail on gable side of first shingle in each row must be 1-1/2 inch from edge of shingle.

Be sure the nails go into but not through the sheathing.

CAUTION

To avoid crushing the wood around a shingle nail, **do not** hit nail after head of nail [8] is flush with surface [7] of shingle. Crushed wood [6] can decay early.

3. Using nails which will go into but not through the sheathing, nail shingle in place with two nails [3].

The second shingle [7] is installed at the other end of the course. The procedure depends upon whether the course ends at a gable edge, hip, valley or vertical wall.

4. **If course ends at a gable edge,** place second shingle [7] with side extended 1/2 to 3/4 inch (1 inch for shakes) beyond gable molding and butt end extended 1-1/2 inches beyond sheathing.

    If course ends at a hip, cut and place shingle strip to fit along hip or hip board.

    If course ends at a valley, place second shingle 6 inches from the valley chalk line made earlier.

    If course ends at a vertical wall:

    a. Install flashing using instructions on Page 25.

    b. Cut and place shingle to fit along wall.

5. Using nails which will go into but not through sheathing, nail second shingle [7] in place with two nails.

6. Nail chalk line [2] to butt ends [5] of shingles at each end of roof.

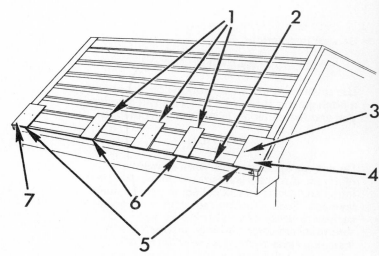

The chalk line is flexible and cannot be used to align all the shingles in the starter course. It is used to align a few shingles. The other shingles are aligned to the first few shingles.

Do not use shingles less than 4 inches or more than 8 inches wide at butt end.

7. Nail several shingles [1] between the two end shingles [4,7] with butt ends [6] on the chalk line [2]. Use two nails [3] per shingle.

The gap [2] between shingles allows shingles to swell without buckling when they get wet.

8. Install additional shingles [11] between shingles [8] installed earlier, but review a, b, c, and d below.

    a. Allow a 1/4 inch gap between shingles.

    b. Using shingling hatchet, split shingles [1] as necessary.

    c. Use board [10] to align shingles [11] with butt ends of nailed shingles [8].

    d. Nail shingles [11] with butt ends in line. Use two nails [9] per shingle.

9. Complete starter course.

10. Remove chalk line.

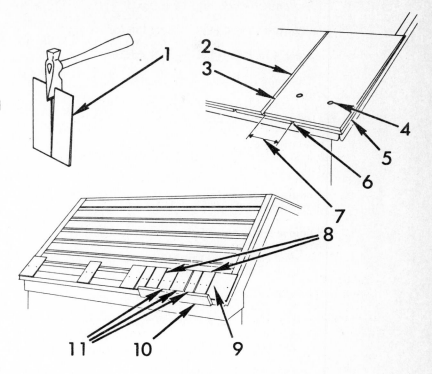

▶ **Install First Course**

1. Place first course of shingles [3] **on top of** starter course [5]. Select shingles with width that will make gaps [2] that are offset from gaps [6] in the starter course by at least 1-1/2 inches [7].

2. Nail first course shingles [3] on top of starter course [5] with two shingle nails [4] for each shingle.

▶ **Install Second and Succeeding Courses**

1. Select first shingle [5] with a width that will make 1/4 inch gap [9] offset at least 1-1/2 inches [8] from the gaps [7] on the first course.

2. Set desired exposure [1] on shingling hatchet with adjustable weather exposure gauge [2].

3. Place weather exposure gauge on hatchet against butt ends of first course shingles. Align both sides [6] of butt end of shingle to desired exposure.

Be sure that nails [4] go into the sheathing [3]. Place nails no more than 1-1/2 inches above exposure and 3/4 inch (1 inch for shakes) from sides of each shingle.

4. Nail shingle in place with two nails.

5. Place next shingle on course with 1/4 inch gap [9] between it and installed shingle. Align one corner of butt end [10] with lower corner of installed shingle. Using exposure gauge [1] on hatchet, align other corner [11] of butt end.

6. Nail shingle in place with two nails.

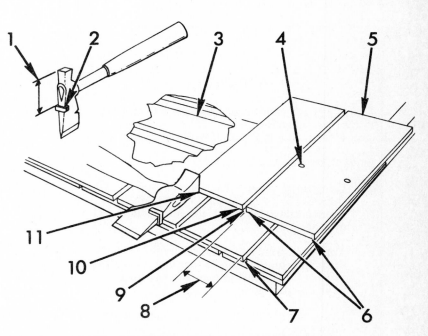

If course ends at a valley, install shingles next to valley before going to Step 7 to complete the second and remaining courses. See instructions on Page 49.

If course does not end at a valley, continue with Step 7.

INSTALLING WOODEN SHINGLES

Install Second and Succeeding Courses

7. Install all but the last shingle, noting the following:

   a.   Make 1/4 inch gaps between all shingles.

   b.   Offset gaps 1-1/2 inches from gaps in first course.

8. Install last shingle in course, noting the following:

   a.   **If course ends at a gable edge,** allow last shingle to extend 1/2 to 3/4 inch (1 inch for shakes) beyond gable molding.

   b.   **If course ends at a hip,** cut and place last shingle to fit along hip or hip board.

   c.   **If course ends at a valley,** cut next to last shingle to fit between shingle next to valley (installed earlier) and third to last shingle, noting the following:

      (1)   Allow 1/4 inch gaps between shingles.

      (2)   Do not cut shingle to a width less than 4 inches. If necessary, cut two shingles to fit.

   d.   **If course ends at a vertical wall,** perform the following:

      (1)   Install flashing using instructions on Page 25.

      (2)   Cut and place shingle to fit along wall.

WARNING

If pitch of roof is greater than 1/3, install cleats to use as steps to prevent you from falling. Build cleats after installing the sixth course. Use instructions below.

9. Continue with remaining courses but note the following:

   a.   Plan shingles so that gaps in three successive rows are offset from each other.

   b.   Make a chalk line after every six courses to check that courses are straight (Page 14).

   c.   When within 5 to 6 feet of roof ridge, adjust course alignment, using instructions on Page 34.

   Use instructions on Page 34 for installing shingles around chimneys or vent pipes.

   Use instructions on Page 49 for installing shingles on hips and ridges.

HOW TO BUILD CLEATS

A cleat [1] is a board nailed to three shingles [2]. In turn the shingles are nailed to the roof. The cleat is then used as a kind of working platform.

Build cleats after every six shingle courses.

a.   Using three nails per shingle, nail three shingles [2] to each cleat [1]. Build as many cleats as necessary for entire length [3] of roof.

b.   Turn over cleat and shingles combination. Place the combination so that upper edge [4] of cleat will be the bottom line [5] for the next shingle course.

c.   Using two nails [6] per shingle, nail shingles [2] onto roof.

d.   When roofing is complete, cut the shingles [2] on each cleat [1] flush with the upper edge [4] of the cleat.

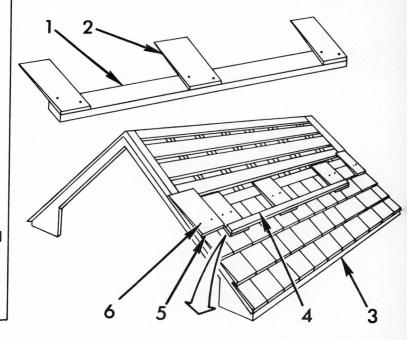

48

Install Shingles Next to Valley

Shingles should not be installed in valleys. Chalk lines made during preparation are the borders for the valley. The shingles should be installed to the chalk lines and not into the valley.

1. Place a shingle [2] 1/4 inch from the nailed shingle [1] closest to the valley. Align butt end [9] of shingle with butt end [10] of nailed shingle.

2. Mark a line [5] on shingle to fit valley chalk line [4]. Cut shingle along the line [5].

Use the cut shingle as a pattern for the next three steps.

3. Stack several shingles in a pile with their butt ends [7] aligned.

4. Nail pile through top ends [6] of shingle to hold them together while sawing.

5. Using fine toothed saw, cut entire pile to match pattern.

6. Nail starter course shingle [2] in place along chalk line. Cut 1-1/2 inch wide strip from first course shingle. Nail first course shingle [3] on top of starter shingle along chalk line.

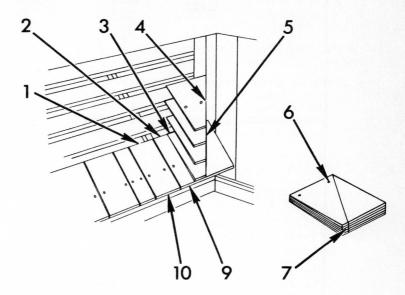

7. Using same exposure as rest of course, nail second and remaining course shingles along chalk line.

Install Hip and Ridge Shingles

Hip and ridge shingles can be bought as prefabricated units [1] or you can make them yourself.

If making hip and ridge shingles, make their width [4] equal to the shingle exposure [2]. Make the length twice the shingle exposure.

When using composition roofing surface materials, be sure the surfaces are **dry.** Moisture can cause the wooden surfaces to decay or be attacked by fungi.

Also, composition roofing materials must be installed in mild weather. Materials may crack when installed in cool weather.

1. Use 8 inch wide strips [7] of 30 lb roll roofing as underlayment for hips and ridges. Nail strips to roof sheathing or ridgeboards. Nails [6] should be 8 inches apart and 1 inch in from each side of strip.

2. Place shingles [8] on hips and ridges. If using two shingles, alternate the lap [3,5] from side to side along hips and ridges.

3. Nail each shingle in place with two rust resistant nails [9] located to be covered by next shingle.

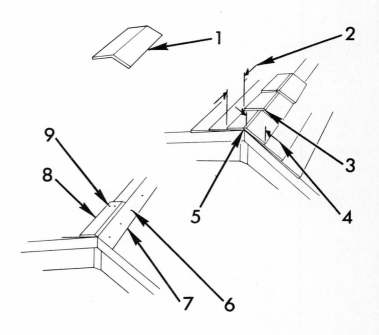

INSTALLING SHAKES

Shakes should not be installed on a roof that had another type of roofing surfacing materials on it. The space [1] between sheathing [2] for shakes differs from that used for wooden shingles.

Use the instructions for installing wooden shingles to install shakes with the following changes:

- Wooden shingles are used for the starter course for shakes as well as for wooden shingles. Thus, when installing shakes, you will have to buy enough wooden shingles to use for the starter courses.

- Since shakes are hand split shingles, the sides are not as straight as the sides of wooden shingles. It will be more difficult to get an exact space or gap [4] between shingles. Therefore, try to make the gap about 1/4 to 3/8 inch.

- Do not use shakes less than 4 inches or more than 8 inches wide.

- When installing the first shake in a course at gable edge, place the shingle 1 inch beyond the gable molding [6].

- Nails should be 1 inch from the sides of each shingle.

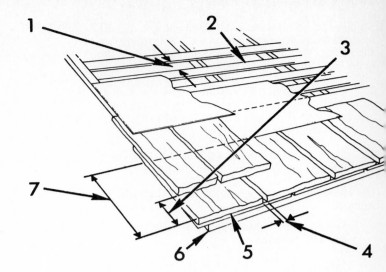

- Install an 18 inch wide strip of 30 lb roofing paper between first and second and succeeding courses of shakes. Paper should cover top of shakes and sheathing above installed course. Distance [7] bottom edge of paper should be from butt [5] is approximately twice the exposure [3] being used to install shakes.

INSTALLING ROLL ROOFING

Each roll of mineral-surfaced composition roll roofing material [1] is 3 feet wide and 36 feet long. It is designed to cover 100 square feet of roof. The excess material is used for 6 inch horizontal laps and 6 inch vertical laps. A standard roll of roofing weighs 87 lbs and is called 90 lb roofing.

To remove old roofing surfacing materials and prepare for roofing installation, use instructions on Page 9 with the following changes:

- Do not install underlayment.
- Do not install eaves flashing strip.

Roofing paper strips can be installed vertically [2] or horizontally [4]. The nails used to install roll roofing may be exposed [3] or concealed [5].

If roof has a pitch of 7/12, the roofing strips should be applied horizontally across the roof. For lower pitched roofs, it will be easier to apply roofing strips vertically. (See Page 7 for definition of pitch.)

If installing strips vertically, most of the work can be done from sheathing, without walking on the roofing surface materials. This reduces the possibility of damaging new roofing materials.

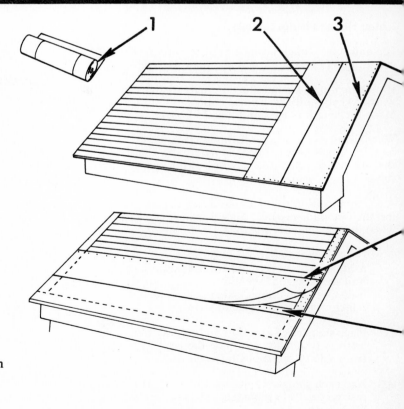

Complete instructions are given for installing roll roofing strips vertically and horizontally. A slightly different procedure is required if the nails are to be concealed. Thus, the necessary changes to the procedures to install the roofing with concealed nails are also provided.

WARNING

Be sure to review the general safety rules before starting.

▶ **Tools and Supplies**

The following tools and supplies are used to install composition roll roofing.

- Roofing knife [1] with a curved end and a very sharp point to cut and fit roll roofing.

- A 2 inch wide paint brush [2] and putty knife to spread roofing lap cement and asphalt roofing cement.

- A chalk line [3] and chalk to mark the roof for proper alignment of roofing materials.

- A carpenter's folding rule [5] and a 50 foot steel tape [4] for making measurements.

- A shingling hatchet [6] or hammer for nailing roofing in place.

- Ladders and scaffolding [7] to provide access to the roof and to support you while working on lower portions of the roof.

- Rolls of 90 lb mineral-surfaced roll roofing [8] which is supplied with suitable roofing cement and 7/8 inch roofing nails.

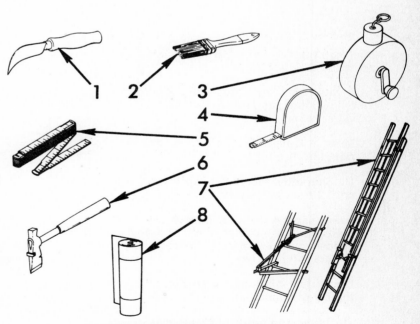

- Molding strips to hold roofing paper to sheathing edges. Select molding with width equal to sheathing thickness at eaves and gable edges of your roof.

- Roofing lap cement and asphalt roofing cement.

INSTALLING ROLL ROOFING

▶ General Instructions

WARNING

Use small seats [1] for yourself and for materials to avoid injury from falls when working on a roof with a pitch greater than 1/4. (See Page 7 for definition of pitch.)

CAUTION

Composition roll roofing must be installed in mild weather. If temperature is too cool, the materials may crack and wrinkles may appear in roofing in warm weather.

Install composition roofing surface materials on dry surfaces only. If materials are installed on damp surfaces, wooden surfaces may decay or be attacked by fungi.

Do not leave strips of roofing on lawn when warming in sun. Absorbed heat will burn lawn.

Do not walk on composition roofing in very hot weather. Damage to roof can occur.

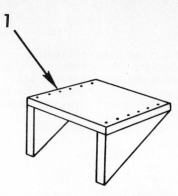

The following procedures describe how to install roll roofing on smooth surfaces. Special instructions on Page 62 show how to install roll roofing around chimneys, vent pipes, and where a roof meets a vertical wall.

Special instructions on Page 56 show how to use two short strips of roofing when installing roll roofing strips vertically and full length strip is unavailable.

Before starting, review special instructions on Pages 56 and 62 first. Then return to this page and continue.

▶ **Install Roll Roofing Strips Vertically with Exposed Nails**

If you would rather have the nails concealed, review instructions on Page 62 before using procedures below.

1. Measure distance [3] from eaves edge to ridge line of roof.

2. Unroll roofing paper. Let paper warm in sun until it becomes pliable.

Cut roofing paper 4-3/4 inches longer than distance [3] measured. This provides for 3/4 inch to turn down over eaves edge [5] of sheathing and 4 inches extended beyond ridge line [1].

3. Use roofing knife and straightedge to cut roofing paper into strips to the length needed.

4. Place first strip parallel to gable edge of roof with strip extended:

    a. 4 inches beyond ridge line [1] of roof.

    b. 3/4 inches beyond eaves edge [5] and gable edge [4].

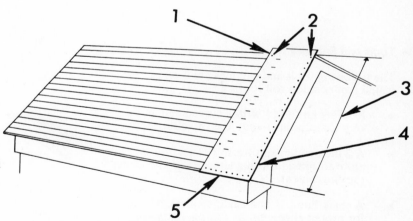

Use 7/8 inch galvanized roofing nails to install composition roll roofing. If nails show through sheathing at eaves overhang, use shorter nails in this area only.

CAUTION

Drive nails straight in to avoid cutting roofing paper with nail heads.

5. Nail top of strip in place with two nails [2]. Place nails 1 inch in from each side of roll roofing strip and 1 inch below ridge line.

6. Nail strip every 2 feet along both sides [3,4]. Be sure paper stays parallel to gable edge of roof.

7. Complete nailing strip in place along gable side [4] and eaves edge [5]. Place nails 1 inch in from edges and 2 inches apart.

8. Mark location of sheathing cracks [1] lightly on roll roofing strip. Make marks [2] 6 inches in from side [3] of roofing strip. Mark lightly so lines are not evident when roof is finished.

9. Place next strip parallel to last strip installed, with strip extended:

   a. 3/4 inch beyond eaves edge [8],

   b. 4 inches beyond ridge line, and

   c. 6 inches beyond edge [7] of last strip installed.

10. Nail top of strip in place with two nails [6]. Place nails 1 inch in from each side of roll roofing strip and ridge line.

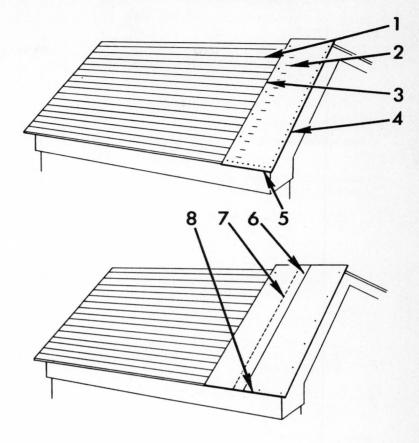

Roofing lap cement must be warm when used. An acceptable method of warming cement is to place can of cement in warm water.

WARNING

Do not heat cement directly over fire. Explosion or fire could occur.

11. Lift edge [1] of roofing strip and apply a 6 inch wide strip of roofing lap cement to edge [2] of last strip of roofing paper installed.

12. Press edge [1] of strip into lap cement.

Refer to sheathing crack marks made earlier to avoid nailing into cracks between sheathing.

13. Nail roofing strip to sheathing. Place nails in vertical row 4 inches apart and 1 inch in from overlapping edge [1].

14. Nail bottom edge [3] of strip. Place nails 2 inches apart and 1 inch up from eaves.

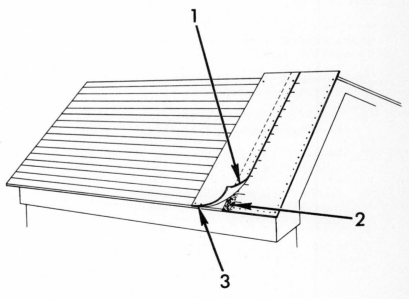

INSTALLING ROLL ROOFING

Install Roll Roofing Strips Vertically with Exposed Nails

15. Repeat Steps 8 through 14 to install all except the last full length strip of roofing.

   If course ends at a valley, go to Step 20 to install last strip.

   If course ends at a hip, go to Step 24 to install last strip.

   If course ends at a gable edge, use Steps 16 — 19 below to install last strip.

16. Place strip on roof as follows:

   a. overlapped 6 inches with last strip installed,

   b. extended 3/4 inches beyond eaves edge [5] of sheathing,

   c. extended 4 inches beyond ridge line [3].

17. Using pencil, mark a line [2] 3/4 inch beyond gable edge [1] on portion of strip that extends past gable edge.

18. Cut strip along line made in Step 17.

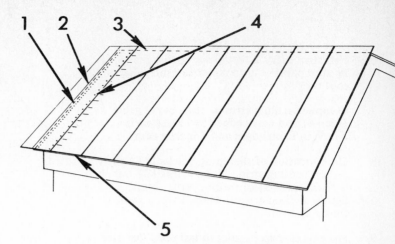

19. Nail strip to sheathing. Place nails as follows:

   a. Two nails 1 inch in from each side of strip and 1 inch below ridge line.

   b. 4 inches apart and 1 inch in from edge of overlap [4].

   c. 2 inches apart and 1 inch in from gable and eaves edges [1,5].

Go to Page 55, bottom, for instructions on how to bend and nail extended edges of roll roofing.

If course ends at a valley, use Steps 20 — 23 below to install last strip [1].

20. Cut roofing strip to fit to valley chalk line [3] made earlier.

21. Apply a 6 inch wide strip of lap cement [4] to valley flashing along chalk line [3].

22. Press roofing strip into lap cement [4] on valley flashing.

23. Nail roofing in place along valley with nails [2] 2 inches apart and 1 inch in from edge of roofing strip.

Go to Page 55, bottom, for instructions on how to bend and nail extended edges of roll roofing.

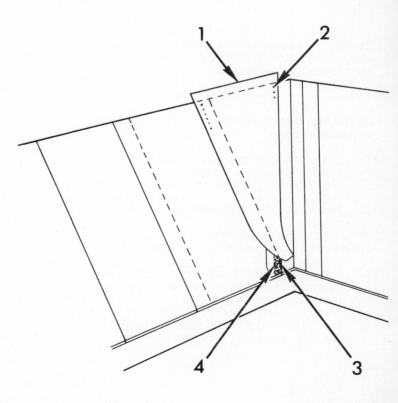

If course ends at a hip, use Steps 24 – 28 below
to install last strip.

24. Measure distances from edge [1] of installed
strip to edge [3] of hip at ridge line [2] and
at eaves edge [5].

 Cut roofing paper 10 inches wider than distances
measured. This provides 4 inches for overlap of
hip and 6 inches for overlap of roofing strip [6].

25. Using roofing knife and straightedge, cut
roofing paper to width needed.

26. Repeat Steps 8 through 14. Then continue.

27. Nail strip to sheathing near edge of hip.
Place nails 1 inch in from edge of hip
(or 5 inches from edge [4] of roofing strip)
and 2 inches apart.

28. Bend roofing strip down over edge of hip.
Nail strip to sheathing. Place nails 1 inch
in from edge [4] of strip and 8 inches apart.

Go to Step 29 for instructions on how to bend and
nail extended edges of roll roofing.

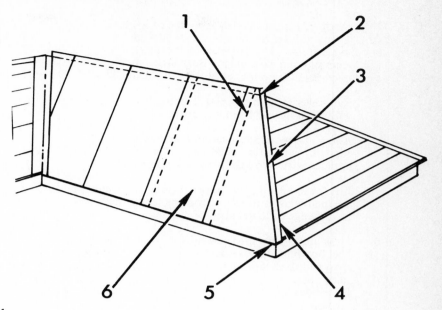

Use Steps 29 – 32 below **to bend and nail extended
edges.**

29. Bend down 4 inches of extended roofing
strips [1] at ridge line. Nail to sheathing
with roofing nails spaced 8 inches apart and
located 1 inch in from edge of strip.

30. Bend down 3/4 inches of extended roofing
strips at gable [2] and eaves [4] edges of
sheathing.

31. Nail to edges of sheathing with roofing nails
spaced 6 inches apart.

Molding strips [3] are used to hold roll roofing
edges to sheathing.

32. Nail molding strips to edges of sheathing.
Use galvanized finishing nails spaced 16 inches
apart.

33. Cover nail heads with asphalt roofing cement.

Use instructions on Page 62 for installing strips
on hips and ridges.

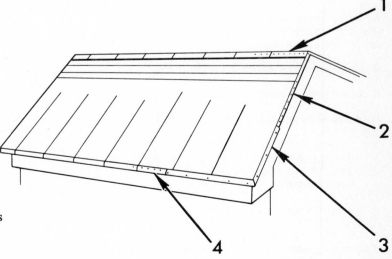

SPECIAL INSTRUCTIONS ON
HOW TO USE TWO SHORT STRIPS
IN PLACE OF FULL LENGTH STRIP

Upper strip [3] must overlap top edge of lower strip [6] by at least 6 inches and extend 4 inches beyond ridge line [1]. Lower strip must extend 3/4 inches beyond eaves edge. Both strips must overlap edge [7] by 6 inches of last strip installed.

a. Nail lower strip in place at sides and eaves with nails spaced 18 inches apart.

b. Allow upper strip to overlap 6 inches at top edge of lower strip. Hold top [4] of strip in place with two galvanized roofing nails.

c. Lift lower edge [2] of upper roofing strip and apply a 6 inch wide strip [5] of roofing lap cement to top edge of lower strip of roofing.

d. Press upper strip into cement on lower strip. Nail bottom edge of upper strip to lower strip and to sheathing with two rows of nails. Start nails 1 inch from bottom edge. Place nails and rows 4 inches apart.

e. Nail sides of strips to sheathing. Locate nails 1 inch in from edges of sheathing 2 inches apart or 1 inch in from edge of next to last strip installed and 4 inches apart.

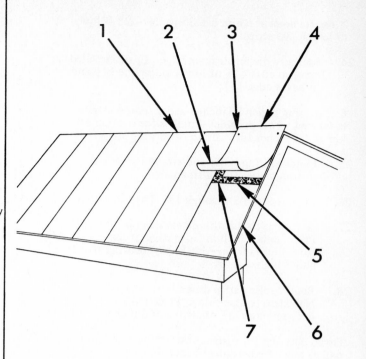

▶ **Install Roll Roofing Strips Horizontally with Exposed Nails**

Be sure to read General Instructions on Page 52.

When installing horizontally with exposed nails, first strip of roll roofing will be installed along eaves edge [3] of roof.

If course ends at a valley, go to Step 14.

If course ends at a hip, go to Step 28.

If course ends at a gable edge, start with Steps 1 – 13 below.

1. Measure horizontal distance from gable edge [1] to gable edge [3]. Record measurements.

2. Unroll roofing paper and let it warm in sun until it becomes pliable.

Cut roofing paper 1-1/2 inches longer than distance measured. This provides 3/4 inches at each end to turn down over end of sheathing at gable edge.

3. Using roofing knife and straightedge, cut roofing paper to length needed.

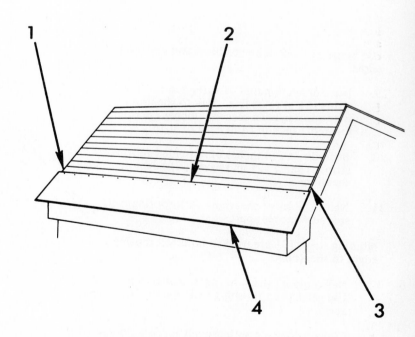

4. Starting at eaves edge of roof, locate first strip [2] parallel to eaves edge of roof. Extend strip 3/4 inches beyond eaves edge [4] and gable edges [1,3].

Avoid hammering nails into cracks [1] between pieces of sheathing. Use 7/8 inch galvanized roofing nails to install composition roll roofing. If nails show through sheathing at eaves overhang, use shorter nails in this area only.

CAUTION

Drive nails straight in to avoid cutting roofing paper with nail heads.

5. Nail top edge of strip to sheathing with nails placed 18 inches apart.

6. Nail sides and lower edge of strip to sheathing. Place nails 2 inches apart and 1 inch in from edge [2] of sheathing or 1-3/4 inch in from edge [3] of roll roofing.

7. Cut second strip of roofing. Place it parallel to first strip with a 6 inch overlap [5] of first strip. Extend strip [6] 3/4 inches over gable edges.

8. Nail top edge of second strip to sheathing with nails placed 18 inches apart.

9. Using pencil, lightly mark location of lower edge [4] of second strip on first strip.

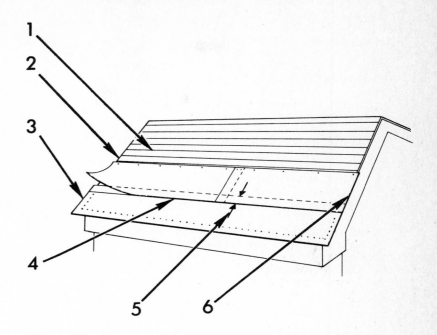

Roofing lap cement must be warm when used. An acceptable method of warming cement is to place can of cement into warm water.

WARNING

Do not heat cement directly over fire. Explosion or fire could occur.

10. Lift lower edge [3] of second strip. Using pencil mark as guide, apply a 6 inch wide strip [7] of lap cement to top edge of first strip.

11. Press second strip into lap cement.

12. Nail strip to sheathing. Place nails 4 inches apart and 1 inch up from bottom edge [4] of second strip. Place nails 2 inches apart along sides of strip at gable edges 1 inch in from edge [1] of sheathing or 1-3/4 inch in from edge [2] of roll roofing.

If using more than one piece of roofing in any horizontal strip, use following procedure:

    a. Use a 6 inch overlap [6] where pieces meet.

    b. Use a 6 inch wide strip of roofing lap cement to seal overlap.

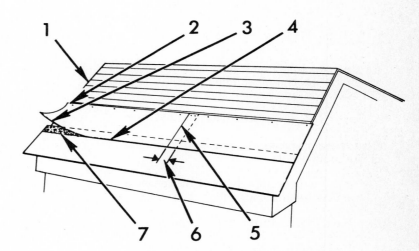

    c. Nail overlap with two rows of nails.

    d. Place nails 2 inches apart in two rows. Locate one row 1 inch from edge [5] of strip and other row 5 inches from edge of strip.

13. Repeat Steps 7 through 12 to install all the roofing strips except the last strip at roof ridge.

Go to Page 61 to install last strip of roof ridge.

INSTALLING ROLL ROOFING

*Install Roll Roofing Strips Horizontally with
Exposed Nails*

If course ends at a valley, use Steps 14 – 27 below.

The first roll roofing strip that ends at a valley
must be cut to fit along the valley chalk line [5].
It must be long enough to extend 3/4 inch beyond
gable edge [1] when it is aligned to extend 3/4 inch
beyond sheathing at eaves edge [4].

14.　Unroll roofing paper for first strip and let
　　　it warm in the sun.

15.　Cut first roofing strip and locate it on roof
　　　to fit along valley chalk line and extended
　　　3/4 inch at gable and eaves edges.

Avoid hammering nails into cracks [2] between
pieces of sheathing. Use 7/8 inch galvanized
roofing nails to install composition roll roofing.
If nails show through sheathing at eaves overhang, use shorter nails in this area only.

CAUTION

**Drive nails straight in to avoid cutting roofing
paper with nail heads.**

16.　Nail top edge [3] of strip to sheathing with
　　　nails placed 18 inches apart.

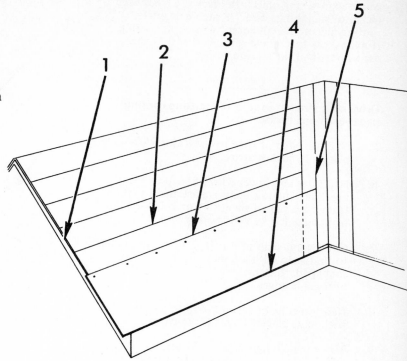

Roofing lap cement must be warm when used. An
acceptable method of warming cement is to place
can of cement into warm water.

WARNING

**Do not heat cement directly over fire. Explosion
or fire could occur.**

17.　Apply 6 inch wide strip [4] of lap cement to
　　　valley flashing along valley chalk line.

18.　Press roofing strip into lap cement.

19.　Nail roofing in place with nails 2 inches
　　　apart and 1 inch in from edge [5] of roofing
　　　strip along chalk line.

20.　Nail gable side [2] and eaves side [3] of
　　　strip to sheathing. Place nails 2 inches apart
　　　and 1 inch in from edge [1] of sheathing or
　　　1-3/4 inch in from side [2] of roll roofing.

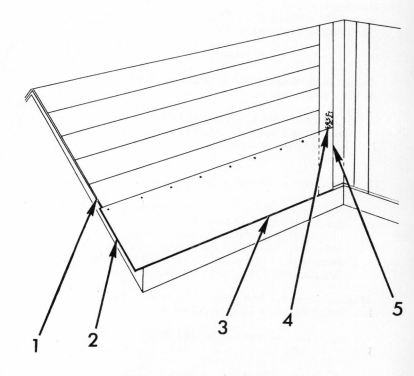

21. Cut next strip of roofing and locate it parallel to installed strip with a 6 inch overlap [3] of installed strip.

22. Nail top edge [1] of strip in place with nails spaced 18 inches apart and 1 inch in from edge.

23. Using pencil, lightly mark location of lower edge [5] of strip on installed strip.

24. Lift lower edge [2] of strip. Using pencil mark as guide, apply a 6 inch wide strip [8] of lap cement to top edge of installed strip.

25. Press lower edge of strip into lap cement.

26. Nail strip in place with nails 2 inches apart and 1 inch up from lower edge [2] of strip. Avoid cracks [4] between sheathing. Place nails along side of strip at gable edge 1 inch in from edge [9] of sheathing or 1-3/4 inch in from edge of roll roofing.

If using more than one piece of roofing in any horizontal strip, use following procedure:

a. Use a 6 inch overlap [6] where pieces meet.

b. Use a 6 inch wide strip of roofing lap cement to seal overlap.

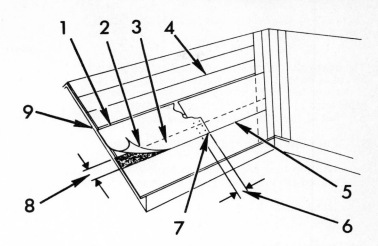

c. Nail overlap with two rows of nails.

d. Place nails 2 inches apart in two rows. Locate one row 1 inch from edge [7] of strip and other row 5 inches from edge of strip.

27. Repeat Steps 21 through 26 to install all the roofing strips except the last strip at roof ridge.

Go to Page 61 to install last strip at roof ridge.

If course ends at a hip, use Steps 28 − 39 below.

28. Unroll roofing paper and let it warm in sun.

The first roll roofing strip that ends at a hip must be cut to extend 4 inches beyond the hip line [3]. It must be long enough to extend 3/4 inch beyond gable edge [1] when it is extended 3/4 inch beyond eaves edge [5] of sheathing.

29. Cut roofing strip and place it on roof.

Avoid hammering nails into cracks [2] between pieces of sheathing. Use 7/8 inch galvanized roofing nails to install composition roll roofing. If nails show through sheathing at eaves overhang, use shorter nails in this area only.

CAUTION

Drive nails straight in to avoid cutting roofing paper with nail heads.

30. Nail top edge [6] of strip to sheathing with nails spaced 18 inches apart.

31. Bend end [4] of roofing strip down over hip line. Nail to sheathing with nails 4 inches apart and 1 inch in from end of roofing strip.

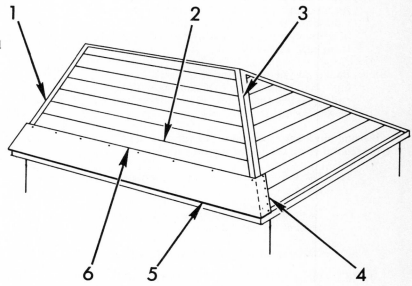

INSTALLING ROLL ROOFING

Install Roll Roofing Strips Horizontally with Exposed Nails

The next roll roofing strip that ends at a hip must be cut to extend 4 inches beyond the hip line [4]. It must be long enough to project 3/4 inch beyond gable edge [1] when it is extended to overlap 6 inches of top edge [5] of installed strip.

32. Cut roofing strip and locate it on the roof.

33. Nail top edge [3] of strip in place with nails spaced 18 inches apart and 1 inch in from edge.

34. Using a pencil, lightly mark location of lower edge [2] of strip on installed strip.

Roofing lap cement must be warm when used. An acceptable method of warming cement is to place can of cement into warm water.

WARNING

Do not heat cement directly over fire. Explosion or fire could occur.

35. Lift lower edge [2] of strip. Using pencil mark as guide, apply a 6 inch wide strip [6] of lap cement to top edge of installed strip.

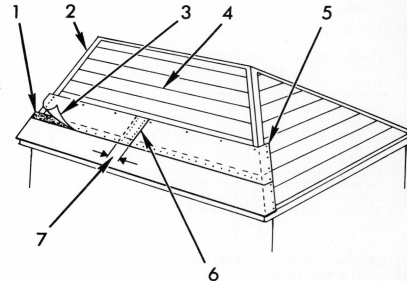

36. Press edge [3] of strip into lap cement [1].

37. Nail strip in place with nails 2 inches apart and 1 inch up from lower edge [3] of strip. Avoid cracks [4] between sheathing. Place nails along sides of strip at gable edges 1 inch in from edge [2] of sheathing or 1-3/4 inch in from edge of roll roofing.

38. Bend end [5] of roofing strip down over hip line. Nail roll roofing to sheathing with nails 4 inches apart and 1 inch in from end of roofing strip.

If using more than one piece of roofing in any horizontal strip, use following procedure:

    a. Use a 6 inch overlap [7] where pieces meet.

    b. Use a 6 inch wide strip of roofing lap cement to seal overlap.

    c. Nail overlap with two rows of nails.

    d. Place nails 2 inches apart in two rows. Locate one row 1 inch from edge [6] of strip and other row 5 inches from edge of strip.

39. Repeat Steps 21 through 26 to install all the roofing strips except the last strip at roof ridge.

Continue on next page to install last strip at roof ridge.

If course ends at a roof ridge, use Steps 40 – 46 to install last strip.

Roll roofing strips that extend to roof ridge line should project up to 4 inches beyond ridge line.

40. Cut a strip of roll roofing to the proper length and locate it parallel to previous strip. Allow strip of roll roofing to overlap previous strip by 6 inches [5].

41. Temporarily nail roll roofing strip in place with nails [1] spaced 4 feet apart and located 3 inches below ridge line of roof. Hammer nails only halfway in.

42. Using a straightedge and pencil, mark a line [2] along roll roofing strip 4 inches [4] beyond roof ridge line [3].

43. Remove nails installed in Step 41.

44. Using roofing knife, cut roll roofing strip along line marked in Step 42.

45. Locate roll roofing strip on roof and nail in place. If strip ends at a valley chalk line, use roofing lap cement along valley chalk line (Page 58, Step 17). Be sure to put nails through holes in roofing made earlier in Step 41.

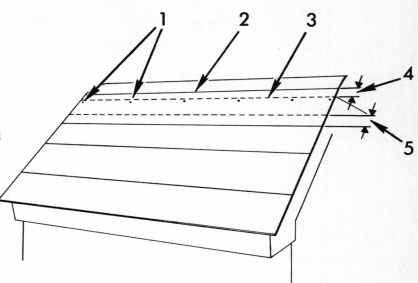

46. Bend projecting 4 inches [4] of roofing strip down across roof ridge line and nail strip to sheathing. Place nails 8 inches apart and 1 inch in from edge of strip.

Use Steps 47 – 50 **to bend and nail extended edges.**

47. Bend extended edges down at gable edge [3] and eaves edge [1] of sheathing. Cut notch [2] at corner of strip.

48. Nail roofing to edges of sheathing with roofing nails [6] at 6 inch intervals.

Molding strips [4] are used to cover and protect roll roofing at edges of sheathing.

49. Nail molding strips to edge of sheathing with nails [5] placed 16 inches apart.

50. Apply daubs of asphalt roofing cement to all exposed nail heads and the immediately surrounding areas.

Go to Page 62 to finish hips and ridges.

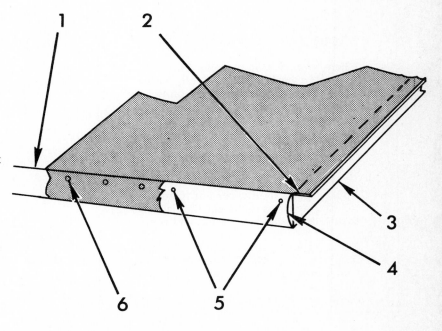

INSTALLING ROLL ROOFING

▶ **Finish Hips and Ridges**

Ridge finishing strips [2] should be long enough to overlap hip finishing strips [4] at least 6 inches.

When hips meet at a ridge [1], hip finishing strips should be cut to meet at ridge line [3].

When hips meet to form a peak [5] instead of a ridge, make the hip finishing strips long enough to overlap the peak at least 4 inches. Use tin snips to cut and fit material to overlay intersecting ridges.

1. Using roofing knife and straightedge, cut 12 inch wide strips of roll roofing as finishing strips for hips or ridges to length needed.

2. Allow roofing to warm in sun before bending it along its centerline to fit over hips or ridges.

3. Using paintbrush, apply a 2 inch wide strip of roofing lap cement [6] under each side of a hip or ridge strip [2,4].

4. Place strip in position. Press strip into roofing lap cement.

5. Nail strip to sheathing with roofing nails. Place nails 1 inch in from each side of strip and 2 inches apart.

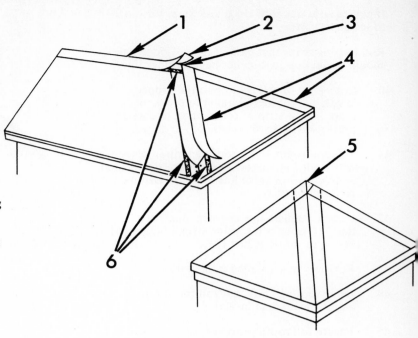

6. Cover nail heads with daubs of asphalt roofing cement or roofing lap cement.

7. Repeat Steps 1 through 6 for all hips or ridges.

SPECIAL INSTRUCTIONS ON HOW TO INSTALL ROLL ROOFING AROUND CHIMNEYS AND VENTS

a. Where roof has chimney and vent flashings or meets a vertical wall, cut roll roofing strips to cover all flashings [1] on the surface of the roof.

b. Apply asphalt roofing cement to entire exposed surface of flashings [1] on surface of roof. Press roll roofing strips into cement on flashings.

c. Apply asphalt roofing cement to edges of roll roofing strips that meet the flashings [2] at surface of chimneys, walls, and vents.

d. Nail roll roofing strips to sheathing through flashings. Place nails 2 inches apart and 1 inch from edge of roll roofing strips.

e. Apply asphalt roofing cement to nail heads.

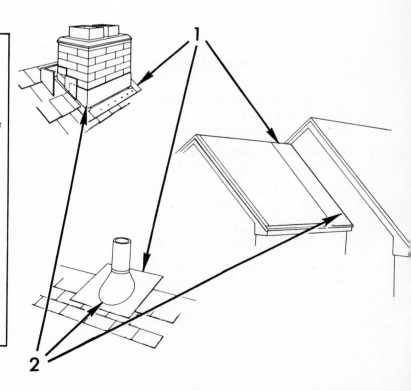

▶ Concealing Roofing Nails

In areas that have little or no wind, roll roofing can be installed with concealed nails.

Instructions below show how to adjust the installation to conceal the nails.

1. Nail 6 inch wide strips [4] of roll roofing to the gable edges, eaves edges, hips, and ridges of the roof. Place nails 4 inches apart and 1 inch in from edge of strip.

2. Install roofing in the same manner as exposed nail roofing except nail strips only at top edges [2] and side edges [3] that do **not** lie above the 6 inch wide strips [4].

3. Apply roofing lap cement to the 6 inch wide strips [4] installed in Step 1 and to 6 inch wide strips [1] along the edges of any strips previously installed. Press all edges firmly into roofing lap cement.

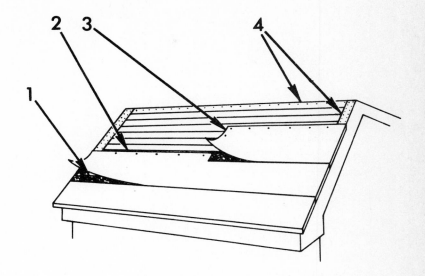

ROOF REPAIRS

The sooner leaks are found and repaired, the less damage there will be. Obvious leaks can be found by a visual check, and can have any of the following causes:

- A house settles at a different rate than a chimney, causing flashing [4] to pull away from chimney or roof.

- Caulking or roofing cement [3] dries out and cracks.

- Flashing [5] corrodes.

- Heat causes asphalt or tar [1] to crack or to blister and break.

- Heat and cold cause various parts of roof and flashings to expand and contract at different rates, tending to pull sealed joints [6] apart.

- Wood [2 or 7] decays or is attacked by fungi.

- Wind, storms, or flying objects cause damage.

Understanding these causes of leaks will help you to make a more effective visual check for leaks.

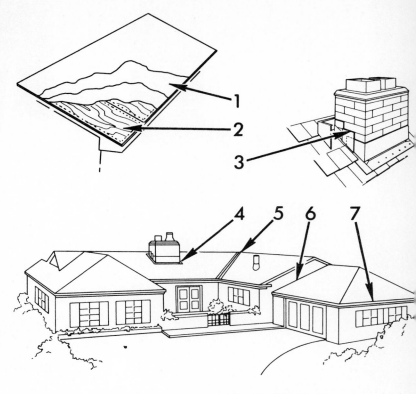

For a thorough visual check, check the following for the types of problems described on the previous page:

- Check for split, cracked, rotted or missing shingles. (This check may be made from underside of roof by looking for opening in shingles. Pinpoint shafts of light through a wooden shingled roof do not necessarily mean roof leaks.)

- Check rock and gravel roofs and other roll roofing for erosion of roofing paper and for cracks or blisters in tar or asphalt.

- Check for broken tiles, slates, or asbestos cement shingles.

- Check flashing [6] and caulking around vents and ventilators.

- Check chimney flashings [4] and caulking [3].

- Check valley flashings [5] for splits or separations.

- Check flashings around skylights.

- Check top of chimney [1] for cracks.

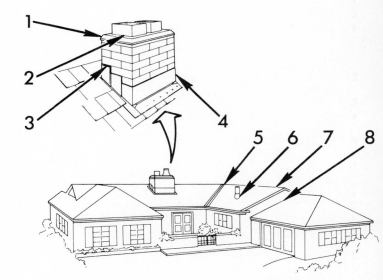

- Check to be sure that joint [2] between flue liner and chimney cap is sealed.

- Check roof ridge line [7], which is especially subject to wind erosion.

- Check joints [8] where porch roofs and garage roofs are attached to wall of house.

When water damages a ceiling, the leak [2] in the roof may not be directly above where the water marks the ceiling [1]. Water can enter through a leak, run down sheathing or rafters and then drip to an attic floor or a ceiling. Such leaks are easiest to find during a storm. Proceed as follows:

1. Take a flashlight or other portable light and go up into the attic. Move to the general location of the leak.

To locate a leak it may be necessary to remove insulation batts [3] or check them for dampness.

2. Find where water makes its entry. Mark the location carefully with chalk or nails.

Another kind of leak that can cause damage is the dripping of water on or behind fascia boards [6]. Such leaks are also easiest to find during storms. So at this time check eaves [5] and roof over-hang [4] for leaks.

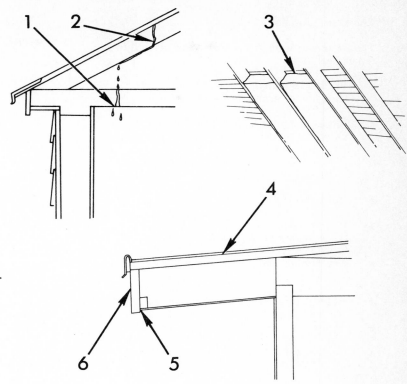

First, locate the leak inside. When the roof has dried out, try to find the leak on the outer surface of the roof.

CAUTION

Do not climb on a wet roof.

Do not walk on composition roofing in very hot weather. Damage to roofing can occur.

Place weight on two or more tiles, slates, or asbestos cement shingles to prevent cracking tiles, slates, or shingles.

Do not assume that water enters roof on outside directly above where it drips on inside. Sometimes water will run between layers of roofing or under flashings.

In order to find a point on the outside which corresponds to the point on the inside of the roof found earlier, reference points are useful. Points on the inside of a roof that can easily be found on the outside of a roof are:

● corner [1] of chimney

● vent pipe [2]

● corner [3] or end of house

● rafters [4]

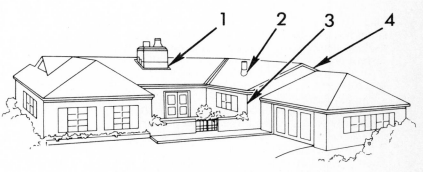

Using such reference points, proceed as follows:

1. Measure distances on inside of roof from known points to point where water enters building.

2. Measure distances found in Step 1 from known points on outside of roof and mark location at which water enters building.

3. Carefully examine exterior of roof for leaks in area close to location marked in Step 2.

Depending on the kind of roof you have and the kind of damage you find, different repair work will be required. The list of repairs on Page 65 will help you find the appropriate procedure for your repairs.

▶ **Tools and Supplies**

The following tools and supplies are needed to repair flashing:

- Pry bar or shingle ripper [1] to remove shingles for access to flashing.

- Sledge hammer [2] and cold chisel [3] to chip loose mortar out of chimney joints.

- Putty knife [4] to apply asphalt roofing cement.

- Tin snips [5] to cut patches.

- 90 lb composition roll roofing material [6] for patching holes and flashing pipes.

- Sheet metal flashing material [7] for patching.

- Asphalt roofing cement [8] and caulking.

- Stiff brush for cleaning area to be repaired.

- Solvent for cleaning area to be repaired.

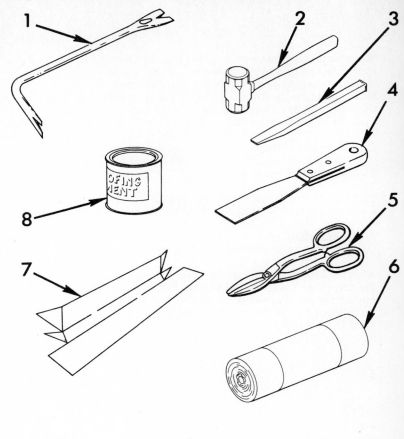

Flashing is used to prevent water from seeping under roofing surface materials wherever the roofing surface slope changes or the roofing surface meets a vertical surface. Typical of these vertical surfaces are chimneys [1], vent pipes [2], and dormers.

Flashing itself can be eroded or corroded. It frequently separates from the surface [3] or surfaces to which it is attached.

There are two possibilities: (1) The flashing damage may be visible and not require removal of shingles. Go to the next page for repair; (2) The flashing damage may not be visible. In this case roofing must be removed to expose the flashing prior to repair. In this case, proceed as follows:

▶ **Removing Shingles**

Exercise care in removing shingles so that they can be replaced undamaged.

1. Using pry bar, lift shingles [4] that cover damaged area.

2. Using shingle ripper or hacksaw blade, remove or cut off shingle nails.

3. Remove shingles [4].

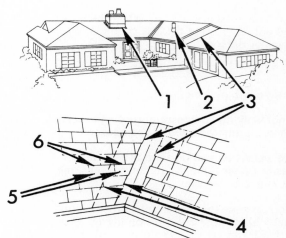

Now make flashing repairs as described on the following pages. Later, shingles will be replaced as described below:

▶ **Replacing Shingles**

1. Install shingles [4] by fastening them in place with nails [5] through next higher course of shingles [6].

2. Apply daub of asphalt roofing cement to any exposed nail heads.

▶ Minor Flashing Repairs

Minor flashing repairs are required for decay or damage which is limited to an area of no more than a few square inches.

Pinholes [1] in metal flashings can be repaired by soldering or by plugging with asphalt roofing cement.

Small holes [3] in either metal or composition flashing can be patched.

Patch [4] should overlap hole [3] on every side by 1 inch.

1. Cut patch [4] from same material as flashing.

2. Using stiff brush and rag soaked in solvent, clean surface to be covered by patch and surrounding area [2].

3. Using putty knife, apply a layer of asphalt roofing cement to surface to be covered by patch and surrounding area [2].

4. Press patch [4] firmly in place and hold temporarily.

5. Release patch and coat entire patch and surrounding area with asphalt roofing cement.

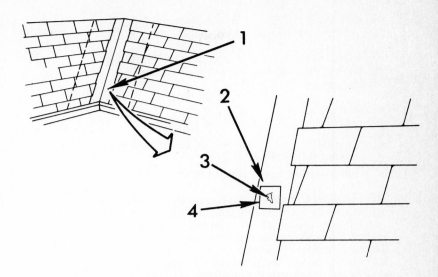

Flashing made of composition roofing materials that have split, blistered, or eroded can be repaired by patching as described above or by sealing with a layer of asphalt roofing.

If shingles were removed to make this repair, go to Page 68 for Replacing Shingles.

Roofing compounds (caulking or sealants) that have dried out are chipped out completely with a hammer and chisel, brushed out and resealed as described below.

If a cap flashing [1] in apparently good condition has pulled away from a chimney, it can be replaced.

1. Using pry bar, carefully pry loose pieces of cap flashing [1] away from chimney. Avoid damaging flashing.

2. Using sledge hammer and cold chisel, chip or scrape loose pieces of mortar out of chimney mortar joints [2].

3. Force caulking or asphalt roofing cement into chimney mortar joints [2].

4. Push cap flashing [1] back into caulking or asphalt roofing cement in mortar joints.

5. Using a heavy object such as a brick, brace flashing until caulking or asphalt roofing cement holds it firmly.

If shingles were removed to make this repair, go to Page 68 for Replacing Shingles.

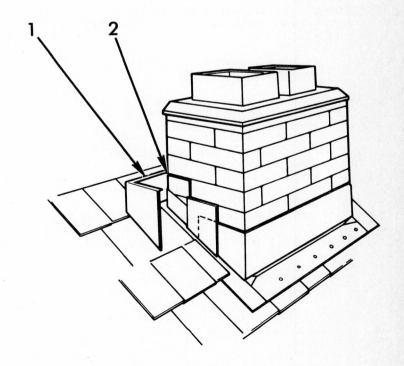

REPAIRING FLASHING

▶ **Major Flashing Repairs**

Major flashing repairs are required when damaged area is larger than a few square inches.

If roofing covering is made from any of the following materials **do not** undertake major flashing repairs. Seek professional help.

- slate
- tile
- decorative rock and gravel on tar or asphalt coated roll roofing
- tar coated layers of composition roll roofing

Major repairs to flashings on other roofing materials are best made by replacing flashings. In some cases, it is necessary to lift shingling or other roofing materials to expose the defective flashing, as described earlier (Page 68). Use care to limit damage to roofing surfacing materials as they are removed to provide access to flashings. Go to Page 12 for instructions for replacing flashings. Read all instructions before starting work.

If leaks occur in a closed valley flashing [1] made of composition roofing materials, it may be possible to temporarily patch the valley. Squares of aluminum or copper are bent to fit into the valley.

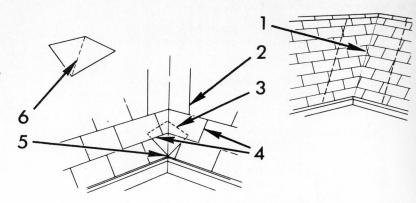

1. Cut 8 x 8 inch squares [3] of aluminum or copper and bend them to fit valley along diagonals [6].

2. Starting at lower end [5] of valley, push 8 x 8 inch squares [3] under shingles [4] and on top of old flashing [2].

3. Repeat Steps 1 and 2, moving up valley past damaged area.

This repair is only temporary and the entire flashing should be replaced in the event that the leak reoccurs.

Procedures for replacing soil stack or vent pipe flashings appear on Page 24. Usually you can buy a prefabricated flashing for this purpose. If not, you can make a flashing from a strip of roll roofing.

1. Measure circumference of pipe by running a piece of string around pipe

2. Cut an 8 inch wide strip of 90 lb roofing paper [1] to a length 4 inches longer than circumference of pipe found in Step 1.

3. Make a series of 3 inch cuts [2] about 2 inches apart along one side of strip.

4. As a trial fitting, wrap roofing paper [1] around pipe with cut edges [3] down and fingers [4] on strip extending onto roofing.

5. Modify cut pattern as needed for a good fit.

6. Using putty knife, coat pipe and roof surfaces to be covered by flashing with asphalt roofing cement [6].

7. Wrap strip of roofing around pipe. Push fingers [4] of flashing into asphalt roofing cement.

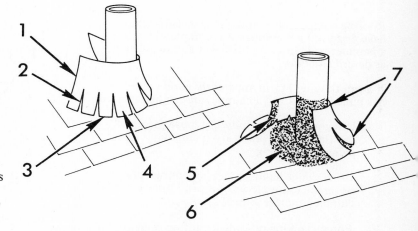

8. Apply asphalt roofing cement to back of flashing overlap [5] and press flashing into place. Nail several fingers [4] to sheathing with galvanized roofing nails. Tie flashing in place until dry.

9. Coat all exposed edges [7] and all exposed nails with asphalt roofing cement.

If shingles were removed to make this repair, go to Page 68 for Replacing Shingles.

Most asphalt shingled roof leaks occur at flashings. Instructions for repairing flashing leaks start on Page 68.

If asphalt shingled roofing is damaged by wind storms, falling branches or other flying objects, one or more shingles may need repair or replacement. If practical, wait for a warm day to make repairs. The asphalt shingles will be more pliable and better repairs can be made.

▶ **Minor Repairs to One or More Shingles**

The following tools and supplies are required:

Putty knife
Shingling hatchet or hammer
Galvanized roofing nails
Asphalt roofing cement

If shingle [2] is partly torn or does not lie flat, proceed as follows:

1. Raise shingle [2] and place daubs of asphalt roofing cement [3] under raised areas.

2. Seal any small tear [1] with asphalt roofing cement.

3. Press shingle [2] into place.

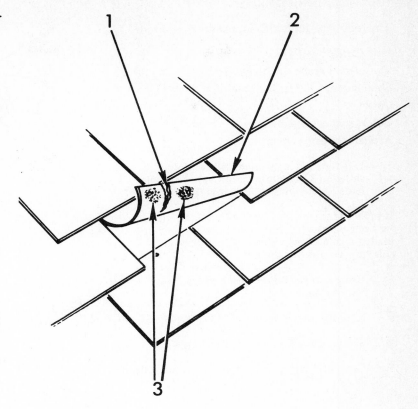

If shingle [1] is badly torn, proceed as follows:

1. Raise shingle [1] and apply layer of asphalt roofing cement to bottom side of shingle and edges of tear.

2. Press shingle [2] down into place.

3. Fasten edges of shingle down with three or four galvanized roofing nails [4].

4. Cover heads of nails with daubs of asphalt roofing cement [3] to prevent leakage at nails.

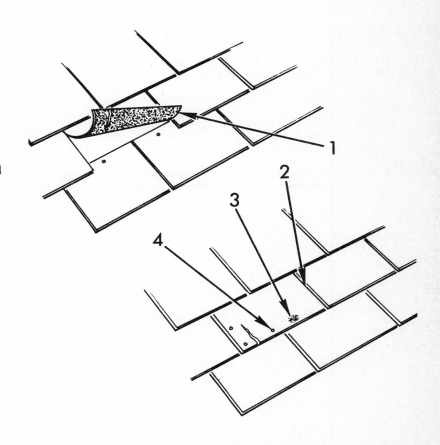

REPAIRING ASPHALT SHINGLED ROOFING

▶ **Replacing Asphalt Shingles**

The following tools and supplies are required:

Putty knife
Flat bladed spade or shingle ripper
Shingling hatchet or hammer
Chisel
Galvanized roofing nails
Asphalt roofing cement

1. Lift tabs [1] of shingles above damaged shingle [3] to permit removal of shingle nails [2] from damaged shingle.

If nails cannot be removed with shingle ripper without damage to adjacent shingles, use flat bladed spade. Insert spade below damaged shingle [3] and pry up nail.

2. Using shingle ripper, pry bar or chisel, remove nails.

3. Remove damaged shingle [3].

4. Slip replacement shingle [5] in place.

5. Fasten replacement shingles [5] to sheathing using galvanized roofing nails [6].

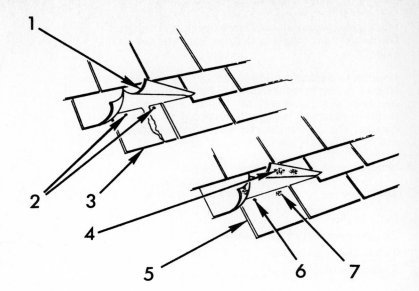

6. Using putty knife, cover heads of roofing nails with daubs of asphalt roofing cement [7].

7. Using putty knife, apply daubs of asphalt roofing cement [4] to underside of tabs [1] on shingles that were lifted to make repair.

8. Press shingles into place.

▶ **Replacing Asphalt Hip or Ridge Shingles**

Damaged hip or ridge shingles are repaired in the same way as regular asphalt shingles. (Page 71.)

To replace hip or ridge shingle, proceed as follows:

1. Lift shingle [1] above damaged shingle [2] to provide access to nails [3] holding damaged shingle.

2. Using shingle ripper or hammer and chisel, remove nails [3] from damaged shingle.

3. Remove damaged shingle [2].

4. Insert new shingle [7] and fasten with four galvanized roofing nails [5].

5. Using putty knife, apply daub of asphalt roofing cement [8] over each nail head [5].

6. Using putty knife, apply large daub of asphalt roofing cement on lower surface [6] on each side of shingle [4] above new shingle [7].

7. Press shingle [4] above new shingle [7] into place.

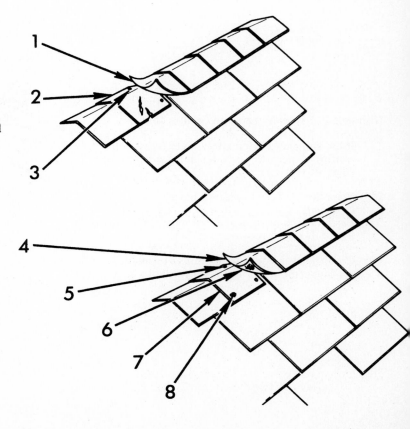

The instructions for repairing wooden shingles can also be used to repair **shakes**. If repairing **shakes**, review instructions for installing shakes on Page 50 then use the following instructions for repairing wooden shingles.

Most wooden shingled roof leaks occur at flashings. Instructions for repairing flashing leaks start on Page 68.

▶ **Replacing Wooden Shingles**

Wooden shingles [2] that have decayed or split, or have been damaged by windstorms or flying objects, should be replaced with new shingles.

The following tools and supplies are required:

Putty knife

Shingling hatchet or hammer and chisel

Shingle ripper [1]

Galvanized 5 penny 1-3/4 inch common nails (2 inch for shakes)

Shingles (or shakes)

Asphalt roofing cement

Scrap board

If shingle ripper [1] is not available you can make one [4] as follows:

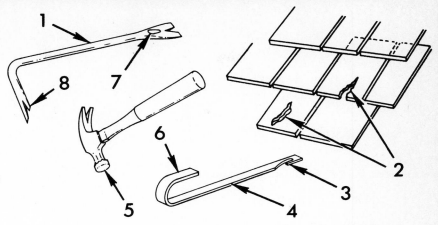

1. Obtain 2 foot piece of 1-1/2 to 2 inch wide strap iron.

2. Cut small notch [3] near one end of strap iron.

3. Bend back other end [6] of strap to provide projection to hammer on when removing nails.

The shingle ripper is used to remove nails, as follows:

Hook notch [3] or slot [7] on shingle ripper over nail shank. Drive nail out with blows from hammer [5] on bent end [6 or 8] of shingle ripper.

Defective shingle [1] can be removed without removing shingle above it.

CAUTION

When removing shakes, be sure not to damage roofing paper installed between shake courses.

1. Using shingling hatchet or hammer and chisel, split defective shingle [1]. Remove separated strips of shingle.

Instead of removing nails with shingle ripper, nails may be cut flush with shingle below, using hacksaw blade.

2. Using shingle ripper, remove nails that held defective shingle in place.

3. Using shingling hatchet [6], trim new shingle [7] to width that allows 1/4 inch gap [3] between new shingle [2] and shingles on each side of it.

A scrap board [10] can be held between shingle butt [9] and hammer [11] while hammering to protect shingle from damage.

4. Tap new shingle [8] into place.

In fastening new shingle [2], nails must pass through shingle [4] above shingle [2] being replaced.

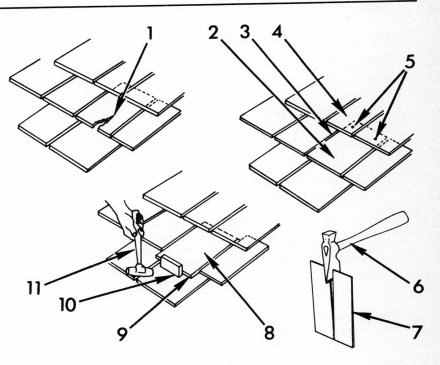

5. Fasten new shingle [2] in place with two galvanized 5 penny nails [5] 1 to 1-1/2 inches above the bottom edge and 3/4 inches in from the side edge of shingle.

▶ **Temporary Repairs**

If a replacement shingle is not available, you can make a temporary repair as follows:

1. Slide 8 x 12 inch sheet metal [1] (aluminum or galvanized steel) below broken shingle [3].

2. Hold sheet metal [1] in place with two galvanized 5 penny nails [2]. Nail through the damaged shingle [3].

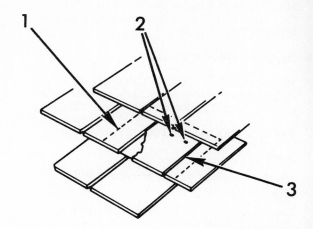

REPAIRING ASBESTOS CEMENT SHINGLED ROOFING

The following tools and supplies are required:

Putty knife

Shingle ripper

Hacksaw blade

Shingling hatchet or hammer and chisel

Center punch

Galvanized nails

Asbestos cement shingles

Asphalt roofing cement or clear butyl cement

Electric drill and drill bits

Most leaks in asbestos cement shingled roofs occur at flashings. Instructions for repairing flashing leaks start on Page 68. Asbestos cement shingles cannot be repaired and must be replaced if damaged.

CAUTION

Asbestos cement shingles [2] are subject to cracking. Place your weight over two or more shingles when walking on roofing.

Asbestos cement shingles are laid in two different patterns. First, procedures will be given for replacing shingles in a Dutch lap pattern. On Page 75, procedures are given for replacing the hexagonal pattern shingles.

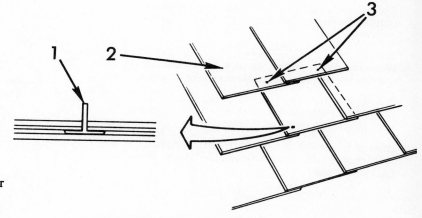

▶ **Replacing Asbestos Cement Shingles in Dutch Lap Pattern**

1. Using shingle ripper, remove nails [3] from defective shingle or use hacksaw blade to cut nails flush with shingle below damaged shingle.

2. Using hacksaw blade, cut through storm anchor shank [1] just below shingle being removed.

3. Remove defective shingle.

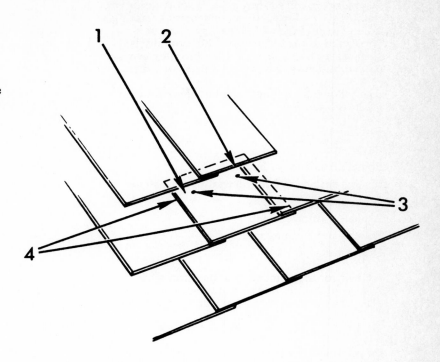

4. Slide replacement shingle [1] in place.

5. Make a mark on surface of replacement shingle with hammer and center punch. Mark surface in two places, 2 inches below butt line [2] of course above replacement shingle and 2 inches in from shingle sides [4].

6. Using electric drill, predrill nail holes [3] through replacement shingle at scored marks. Match drill diameter to other nail holes predrilled in shingles.

7. Nail replacement shingle in place with galvanized steel, stainless steel or aluminum nails through predrilled nails holes [3].

8. Using putty knife, apply asphalt roofing cement or clear butyl cement to nail heads and adjacent area to seal nail holes.

▶ **Replacing Asbestos Cement Shingles in Hexagonal Pattern**

1. Using shingle ripper, remove nails from defective shingle or use hacksaw blade to cut nails flush with shingle below damaged shingle.

2. Remove defective shingle.

3. Slide replacement shingle [1] into place.

4. Using hammer and center punch, make a mark on surface of replacement shingle in two places. Make marks at least 8 inches apart, 2 inches in from edge of shingle, and located to miss other shingles.

5. Predrill nail holes [2] through replacement shingle. Match drill diameter to other nail holes predrilled in shingles.

6. Nail replacement shingle in place with galvanized steel, stainless steel or aluminum nails.

7. Apply coating of asphalt roofing cement or clear butyl cement to nail heads and adjacent area to seal nail holes.

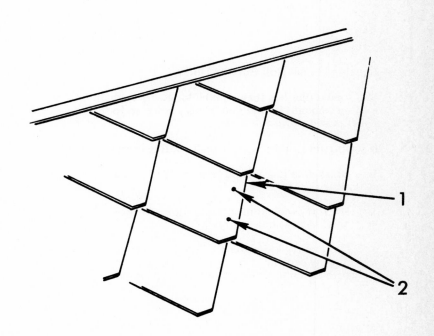

Most leaks in roll roofing covered roofs occur at flashings [2]. Instructions for repairing flashing leaks start on Page 68. Leaks also occur at horizontal seams [1] between horizontally laid strips of roofing. Portions of roll roofing can be eroded or damaged by flying objects or storms.

The following tools and supplies are required to repair roll roofing:

Roofing knife

Putty knife

Shingling hatchet or hammer

Mineral-surfaced 90 lb roll roofing for patches

Galvanized roofing nails

Asphalt roofing cement

Solvent and cleaning rags

Dust brush

Asphalt roofing cement must be warm when used. An acceptable method of warming cement is to place can of cement in warm water.

WARNING

Do not heat cement directly over fire. Fire or explosion could occur.

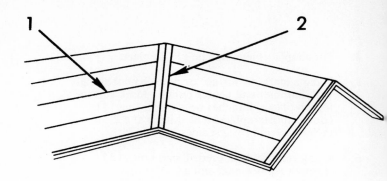

CAUTION

Composition roll roofing must be applied in mild weather. If temperature is too cool, the materials may crack when applied.

Drive nails straight in to avoid cutting roofing paper with nail heads.

Do not walk on composition roofing in very hot weather. Damage to roofing can occur.

► **Repairing Small Roll Roofing Holes**

Seal small holes less than an inch long with asphalt roofing cement [1] and patch small holes up to 2 inches wide with roll roofing.

If sealing small holes with asphalt roofing cement,

1. Brush area [3] around small hole [2] until clean.

2. Using rag soaked in solvent, wipe area around hole. Allow area to dry.

3. Using putty knife [4] fill hole [2] with asphalt roofing cement. Coat surrounding area with a thin layer of asphalt roofing cement.

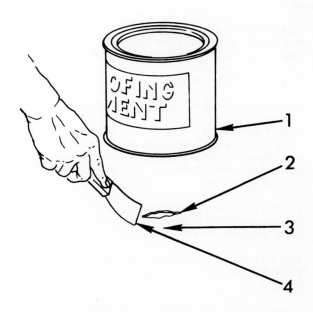

If patching small holes with roll roofing,

1. Brush area [2] around hole [3] until clean.

2. Using rag soaked in solvent, wipe area [2] around hole. Allow area to dry.

3. Using putty knife, fill hole [3] with asphalt roofing cement [1].

4. Cut patch [4] extending 2 inches beyond hole on all sides [5].

Upper side of patch has mineral-coated surface (side with chips).

5. Using putty knife, coat under side of patch [4] with asphalt roofing cement.

6. Press patch [4] into place.

7. Coat patch and surrounding area [6] with asphalt roofing cement.

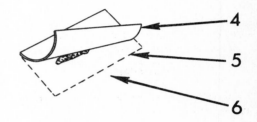

▶ **Repairing Large Holes or Slits in Roll Roofing**

1. Using roofing knife, cut out a square or rectangular piece [2] of roofing that includes defective area [1].

2. With piece [2] that was removed as a pattern, using roofing knife, cut out a patch [3] of roll roofing. Check to see that patch will fit into area roofing was removed from.

3. Brush area to be patched as well as surface of roof extending out about 6 inches on all sides of area.

4. Using rags soaked in solvent, wipe brushed area. Allow area to dry.

5. Using roofing knife, cut another patch [4] of roll roofing that will extend 4 inches beyond first patch on all sides.

6. Using putty knife, coat area [6] to be patched by small patch [3] with asphalt roofing cement [7].

7. Press smaller patch [3] onto asphalt roofing cement [7].

8. Fasten patch [3] in place at four corners with galvanized roofing nails [5].

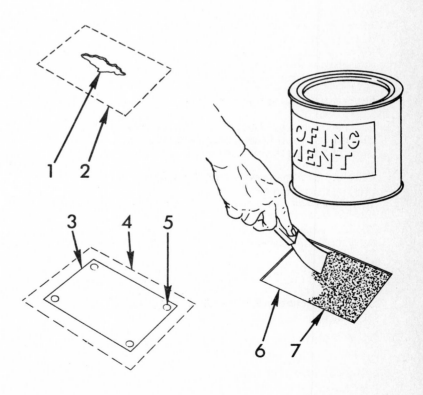

Repairing Large Holes or Slits in Roll Roofing

9. Using putty knife, coat bottom surface of large patch with asphalt roofing cement [1].

10. Press large patch [3] onto roofing above first patch [4]. Nail large patch in place with galvanized roofing nails [2] spaced 2 inches apart and 1 inch in from edge of patch.

11. Using putty knife, coat heads of roofing nails [4] and immediate area with asphalt roofing cement.

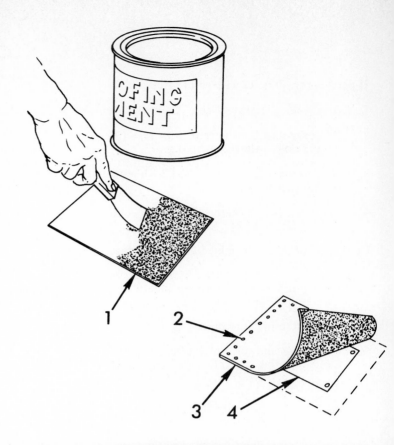

REPAIRING ROCK AND GRAVEL ROOFING

Decorative rock and gravel roofing is made by spreading rock and gravel onto hot mopped layers of tar paper. Rock and gravel roofing leaks when the tar paper [1] is damaged or eroded. The tar or asphalt coating can blister, shrink and crack. As with other roofing, many leaks occur at flashings. For instructions for repairing flashing leaks, go to Page 68.

Damaged areas can be repaired by almost anyone with asphalt roofing cement applied at ambient (surrounding air) temperatures. Major damage will require roofing replacement by a professional roofing firm. The roofing firm will have the equipment and experience needed to hot mop tar onto a roof.

The following tools and supplies are required to repair rock and gravel roofing:

Roofing knife

Putty knife

Shingling hatchet or hammer

60 lb asphalt saturated roll roofing for patches

Galvanized roofing nails

Asphalt roofing cement

Solvent and cleaning rags

Dust brush

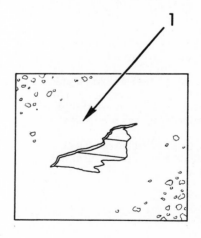

CAUTION

Asphalt saturated roll roofing must be applied in mild weather. If temperature is too cool, the materials may crack when applied.

Drive nails straight in to avoid cutting roofing paper with nails heads.

Do not walk on composition roofing in very hot weather. Damage to roofing can occur.

▶ **Repairing Small Damaged Areas**

If the damaged area [3] is less than 2 inches in length, proceed as follows:

Area brushed should extend 6 inches beyond damaged area in all directions.

1. Brush dirt, rocks, and gravel away from damaged area and surrounding area [1].

2. Using rag soaked in solvent, wipe brushed area [1] clean. Allow area to dry.

Asphalt roofing cement must be warm when used. An acceptable method of warming cement is to place can of cement in warm water.

<u>**WARNING**</u>

Do not heat cement directly over fire. Fire or explosion could occur.

3. Using putty knife, apply asphalt roofing cement [2] to damaged area and surrounding area for a distance of 2 to 3 inches on all sides of the damaged area.

4. Replace gravel and rocks.

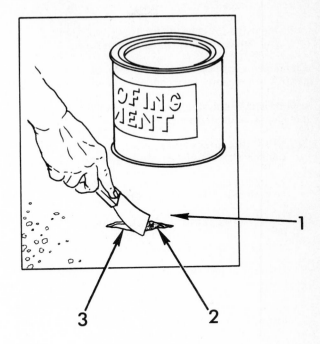

▶ **Repairing Blistered Tar or Asphalt**

If tar or asphalt has blistered, proceed as follows:

Area brushed should extend 6 inches beyond damaged area in all directions.

1. Brush dirt, rocks, and gravel away from damaged area and surrounding area [1].

2. Using rag soaked in solvent, wipe brushed area clean. Allow area to dry.

3. Using roofing knife [2], cut through large blisters.

4. Using putty knife, force asphalt roofing cement under raised portions of blister. Press raised portions of blister flat. Fasten large portions in place with roofing nails [3].

5. Using roofing knife, cut patch [4] of 60 lb asphalt saturated roll roofing to extend 2 inches beyond damaged area on all sides.

6. Using putty knife, coat top of blister and surrounding area with asphalt roofing cement.

7. Press patch [4] of 60 lb asphalt saturated roll roofing into asphalt roofing cement.

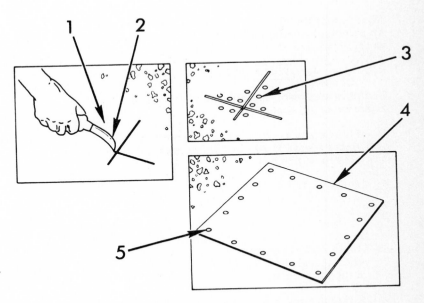

8. Fasten patch in place with galvanized roofing nails [5] spaced 2 inches apart and 1 inch from edges of patch.

9. Using putty knife, cover patch area including nails with asphalt roofing cement.

10. Replace gravel and rocks.

▶ Repairing Large Damaged Areas

Cautions listed on Page 76 for Repairing Small Damaged Areas apply to these instructions.

If damaged area [1] is 2 to 24 inches along its greatest dimensions, proceed as follows:

Area brushed should extend 6 inches beyond damaged area in all directions.

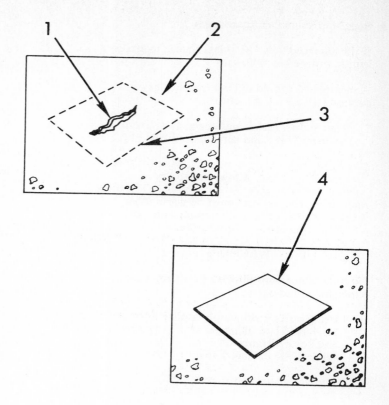

1. Brush dirt, rocks and gravel away from damaged area and surrounding area [2].

2. Using rag soaked in solvent, wipe brushed area clean. Allow area to dry.

3. Using roofing knife, cut out square or rectangle piece [3] of the old roll roofing that includes the damaged area.

4. With piece [3] that was removed as a pattern, using roofing knife, cut out patch [4] of 60 lb asphalt saturated roll roofing. Check to see that patch will fit into the area roll roofing was removed from.

Asphalt roofing cement must be warm when used. An acceptable method of warming cement is to place can of cement in warm water.

WARNING

Do not heat cement directly over fire. Fire or explosion could occur.

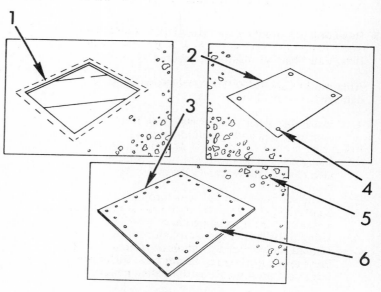

5. Using putty knife, force asphalt roofing cement under edges [1] of old roll roofing around area to be patched.

6. Using putty knife, coat underside of patch with asphalt roofing cement.

7. Press patch [2] in place.

8. Fasten patch [2] in place with four galvanized roofing nails [4], located at the corners 1 inch in from edges.

9. Using roofing knife, cut a second patch [3] of 60 lb asphalt saturated roll roofing 8 inches wider and 8 inches longer than the first patch [2].

10. Using putty knife, coat underside of second patch [3] with asphalt roofing cement.

11. Press second patch [3] in place.

12. Fasten second patch [3] in place with galvanized roofing nails [6] spaced 2 inches apart, 1 inch in from edges.

13. Using putty knife, coat entire patch [3] including nail heads and area surrounding patch for several inches, with asphalt roofing cement.

14. Replace gravel and rocks [5].

The following tools and supplies are required for repairing metal roofing:

Paint scraper

Wire brush

Dust brush

Tin snips

Propane torch and solder

Metal paint primer

Paintbrushes and paint

Asphalt roofing cement

Metal or asphalt saturated roll roofing for patches

▶ **Major Repairs**

Major repairs to metal roofing should be undertaken by a roofing firm.

▶ **Metal Roofing Maintenance**

Roofing on temporary buildings will probably require painting every few years. To paint metal roofing, proceed as follows:

1. Using wire brush and paint scraper, remove loose or peeling paint.

2. Using dust brush, brush roof clean.

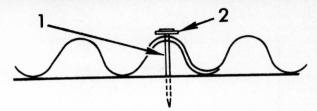

3. Use metal paint primer on rusted and scratched areas.

4. Paint roofing desired color.

▶ **Minor Repairs**

Minor repairs to metal roofing can be made fairly easily.

If roofing must be nailed in place more securely, use galvanized nails [1] with lead washers [2] for galvanized roofing. Use aluminum alloy nails with nonmetallic washers for aluminum roofing.

If there are pin holes in the metal, they can be repaired with solder.

1. Clean area around pin holes with steel wool.

2. Using propane torch and solder, spread melted solder over area with pin holes.

Small patches may be made either with solder and a metal patch, or with asphalt roofing cement and a metal or roll roofing patch.

To make a patch using solder and metal, proceed as follows:

1. Clean area [1] to be patched with steel wool.

Use same material as roofing in preparing patch.

2. Using tin snips, cut metal patch [2] to cover damaged area.

3. Apply acid flux to both underside of patch [2] and area of roof to be patched.

4. Using propane torch, heat areas to be soldered and apply light coating of solder to underside of patch [2] and area of roof to be patched.

5. Press patch in place and apply heat with propane torch to solder patch [2] in place. Check to assure complete solder coverage.

To make a patch using asphalt roofing cement and metal or roll roofing, proceed as follows:

If using metal, use same material as roofing for preparing patch.

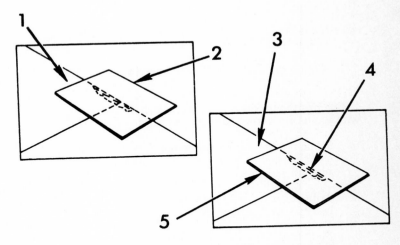

1. Using tin snips, cut patch [5] to cover damaged area [4].

2. Using putty knife, apply asphalt roofing cement to both underside of patch [5] and area [3] of roof to be patched.

3. Press patch [5] in place.

4. Using putty knife, apply asphalt roofing cement to patch and immediate area.

▶ **Major Repairs to Slate Roofing**

Major repairs to slate roofing should be undertaken by a roofing firm.

If repairs to slate shingles or flashing require removal and replacement of more than a few shingles, a roofing firm should do the work.

▶ **Minor Repairs to Slate Roofing**

The following tools and supplies are needed for minor repairs to slate roofing:

Putty knife

Shingle ripper or hacksaw blade

Shingling hatchet or hammer

Center punch

Chisel and straightedge

Electric drill

Replacement slate shingles and galvanized roofing nails

Asphalt roofing cement or clear butyl cement

If flashing repairs are required, go to **Page** 68.

If slate shingle removal and replacement is required due to damage to a few slates or flashing, proceed as follows:

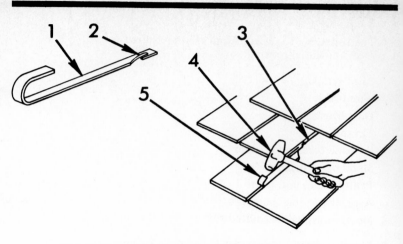

If unable to obtain or make shingle ripper [1] for Step 1 that follows, use hacksaw blade to cut nails flush with shingle below shingle being removed.

If using shingle ripper [1] to remove nails from a slate shingle [3],

1. Hook notch [2] in shingle ripper onto nail under shingle [3].

2. Drive nail out by hitting shingle ripper [5] with hammer [4] or shingling hatchet.

3. Remove shingle [3].

To cut replacement slate shingle to size,

4. Using chisel and straightedge, scratch surface of shingle [2] with chisel [1].

5. Align scratch mark [4] with edge [5] of work bench.

Giving unsupported part of shingle a sharp crack with hand or hammer handle will snap it off.

6. While holding supported part [3] of slate shingle, snap off unneeded, unsupported portion [6] of shingle.

7. Trim edges [7] of slate shingle by tapping lightly with hammer [8].

8. Slide new shingle [9] into place.

9. Make marks [10] on surface of new shingle with hammer and center punch in two places. Make marks 1 inch below butt line of next higher course of shingles [11] and 2 inches in from sides of shingle.

10. Using electric drill, predrill nail holes at score marks [10] through shingle and through shingle below new shingle.

11. Remove new shingle.

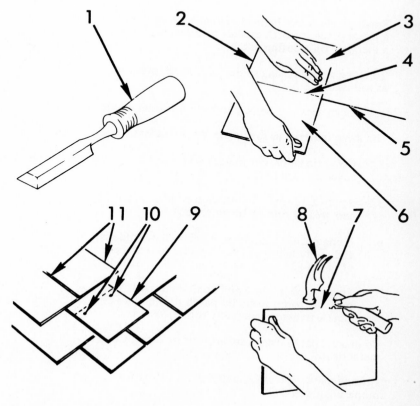

12. Using putty knife, coat underside of shingle [1] with asphalt roofing cement [2].

13. Slide new shingle [3] into place again.

14. Nail new shingle in place with galvanized aluminum or stainless steel nails through predrilled holes [4].

15. Using putty knife, apply coating of asphalt roofing cement or clear butyl cement to nail heads and adjacent area to seal nail holes.

▶ **Major Repairs to Tile Roofing**

Major repairs to tile roofing should be undertaken by a roofing firm. If repairs to a tile roof or its flashing require removal and replacement of more than a few tiles, a roofing firm should do the work.

▶ **Minor Repairs to Tile Roofing**

The following tools and supplies are needed:

Shingle ripper or hacksaw blade
Shingling hatchet or hammer
Punch
Electric drill
Replacement tiles and galvanized nails
Asphalt roofing cement or clear butyl cement

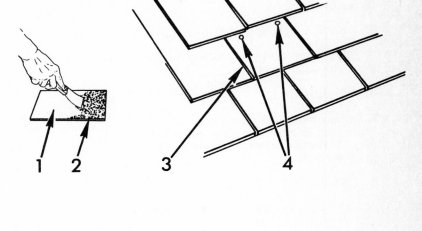

Before you attempt to make any repairs to a tile roof, study the illustrations on this page. This will allow you to determine whether your tiles are mission tiles [1] or spanish tiles [3] before you start work. The instructions for minor repairs to mission tiles are identical to the instructions for minor repair to spanish tiles except that:

● Mission tiles [1] are nailed to a wooden strip [2] called a furring strip.

● Spanish tiles [3] are nailed directly to the sheathing [4].

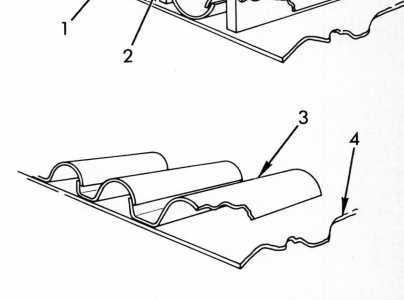

REPAIRING SLATE AND TILE ROOFING

If tile removal and replacement is required due to tile or flashing damage, proceed as follows:

If unable to obtain shingle ripper [8], use hacksaw blade to cut nails flush with furring strip [4] or sheathing below tile being removed.

If using shingle ripper to remove nails from tile to be removed,

1. Hook shingle ripper [8] to nail [3].

2. Drive out nail [3] by hitting shingle ripper [8] with hammer [1].

3. Remove tile [2].

If flashing repairs are required, go to Page 68 Make flashing repairs and then resume this procedure. If flashing repairs are not needed continue the procedure.

4. Slide new tile [9] in place.

5. Using electric drill, predrill nail hole [11] through tile [10] above new tile [9] and new tile. Avoid old nail holes [6].

6. Nail tile in place with galvanized roofing nails [5] and [7].

7. Using putty knife, apply coating of asphalt roofing cement [6] or blear butyl cement to nail heads and adacent area to seal nail hole.

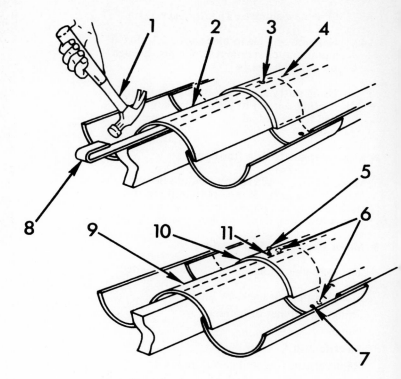

84

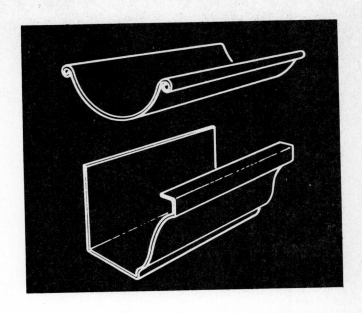

INSTALLING GUTTERS

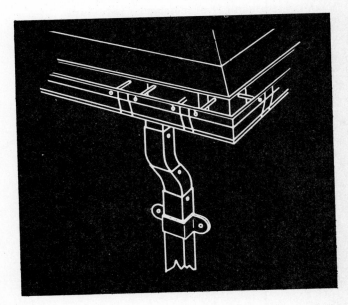

Gutters [1] and downspouts [2] are designed to protect houses from damaging effects of water. Gutters are installed just below the edge of the roof. They collect the water from rain or melted snow and carry it to the downspouts, which guide it to the ground and away from the foundation of the house.

Gutters are made of metal, wood, and plastic. Each material has specific features which affect the installation and the maintenance of gutters. The most important features of each material are described in the following paragraphs.

▶ **Metal Gutters**

The two most commonly used types of metal gutters are galvanized steel and aluminum. Both types are available without finish or with a durable baked enamel finish.

Galvanized steel gutters and downspouts are inexpensive. However, galvanized steel may rust and corrode. Unless it is protected with a rust-preventive primer and painted, the gutter will deteriorate rapidly.

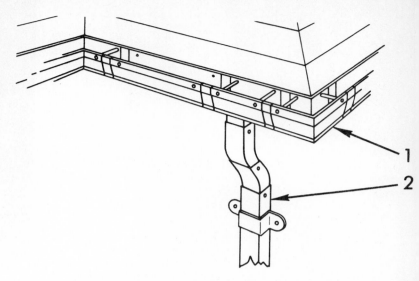

Unfinished aluminum gutters and downspouts are more expensive than those made of steel. Aluminum forms its own protective coating which makes it less susceptible to corrosion. Aluminum is lighter than steel, but aluminum is also weaker and is more easily dented.

Finished steel or aluminum gutters have a durable white enamel finish. The enamel finish eliminates the need for priming and painting. However, the **unfinished** type has the advantage that it can be painted to match the color of the house.

Metal gutters and downspouts are usually available in 10 feet lengths. Gutters may be half-round [1] or formed [2] whereas their corresponding downspouts are round [3] or rectangular [4]. Most downspouts are corrugated to provide additional strength.

Metal gutters are not difficult to install. Both galvanized steel and aluminum gutters are available with all components prefabricated and designed to be easily assembled and joined.

▶ **Plastic (Vinyl) Gutters**

The use of PVC (Polyvinyl Chloride) as gutter material is a relatively new development. Since vinyl will not corrode, vinyl gutters require very little maintenance. However, vinyl will expand when temperature increases. If vinyl gutters are installed without allowing for temperature changes, they will bend or pull away from the roof.

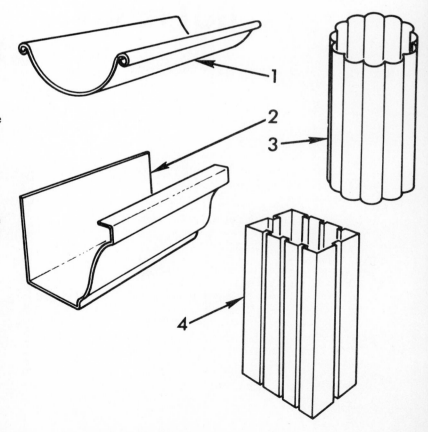

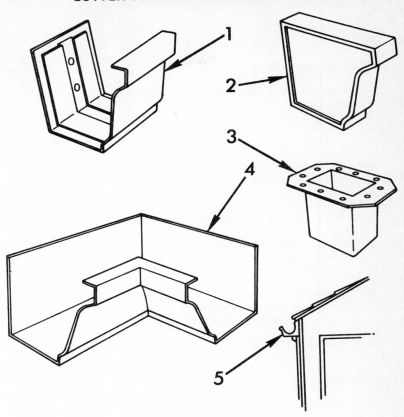

Vinyl gutters are available with preformed connectors [1], end caps [2], preformed corners [4] and drop outlets [3].

▶ **Wooden Gutters**

Wood was once the most widely used gutter material. Occasionally, for decorative purposes, wooden gutters [5] are installed on new houses. On some new houses, wooden gutters [5] are installed as part of the trim.

Wooden gutters require frequent inspection and regular coatings with wood preservatives to prevent rot. However, when correctly installed and properly maintained, wooden gutters may last as long as the house. Replacing or installing wooden gutters require special skills and is a difficult and heavy job. They should be replaced by a carpenter.

▶ **Gutter Fasteners**

Usually gutters are attached with one of the following types of fasteners:

Spike and ferrule fasteners [1]

Bracket hangers [2,3]

Strap hangers [6,9]

Spike and ferrule fasteners [1] are used quite frequently. The spike goes through the front lip of the gutter, through the ferrule, through the back wall of the gutter and into the fascia board. The ferrule keeps the sides of the gutter separated.

Bracket hangers [2,3] are attached to the fascia board or the end of the rafter. Several types are available. The bracket hanger goes around [5] the outside of the gutter or goes across the top [4] and attaches to the lip of the gutter.

Strap hangers [6,9] support the gutter and are attached to the roof sheathing under the shingle. The supporting strap goes around [8] the outside of the gutter or goes across the top [7] and attaches to the sides of the gutter. Avoid the use of strap hangers unless they can be installed before new roofing is installed.

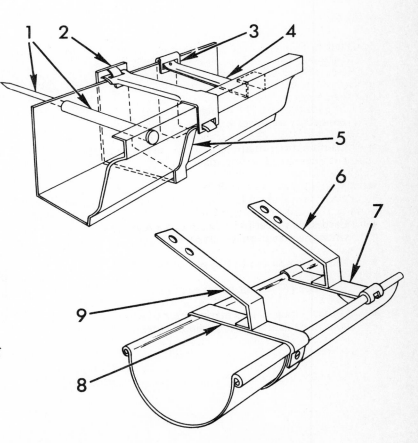

▶ Tools and Supplies

The following tools and supplies are needed to prepare for gutter installation:

- Curved claw hammer [1] to nail gutter to roof or fascia.

- Hacksaw [2] to cut metal gutter sections to correct length.

- Flat single cut file [3] to remove burrs from edges of cut metal gutter sections.

- Electric drill [4] to drill holes in metal gutter sections when using spike and ferrule fasteners.

- Screwdriver, standard [7] or Phillips [5], for installing sheet metal screws to hold downspout sections together.

- Roofing nails [6], large head, galvanized to nail brackets to fascia board.

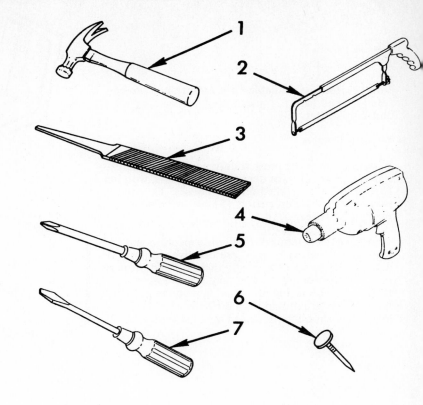

- Slip-joint pliers [1] to bend edges of connector to gutter sections.

- Combination square [2] to help make straight cut lines on gutter sections.

- Straightedge [3] 6 to 8 feet long to make gutter installation line with correct slope.

- Carpenter's level [4] to help make level line when measuring gutter slope.

- Mastic compound [5] to seal gutter joints.

- Tin snips [6] to cut metal gutters.

- Center punch [7] to mark center of spike hole to be drilled through lip of gutter.

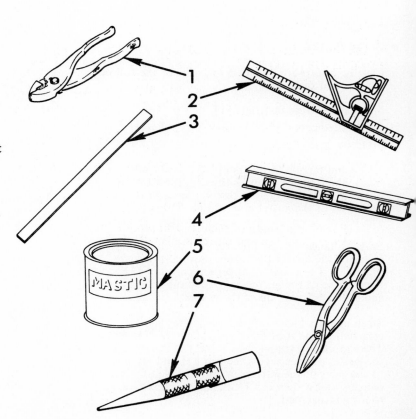

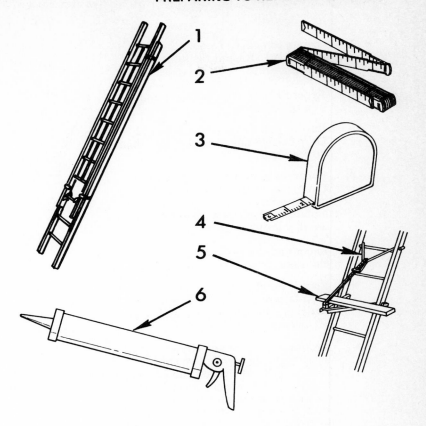

- Ladder [1] to reach edge of roof to install gutters.

- Steel tape [3] or folding rule [2] to measure length of gutter run.

- Ladder hooks [4] and scaffold board [5] to install gutters.

- Wood putty to fill cracks and old nail holes in fascia board.

- Work gloves to protect hands when working with metal gutters.

- Rust-preventive paint primer to cover newly cut edges of metal gutters.

- Caulking gun [6] to seal gutter joints that develop leaks.

▶ **Estimating Material**

Gutters are available in a variety of lengths. However, gutter pieces 10 feet long are generally used because they are easy to install. A piece 10 feet long can be cut to a shorter length as needed to complete a section of a gutter run.

A gutter run may consist of one or more straight sections of gutter.

When replacing gutter runs, draw a diagram of the existing gutter runs before you remove them.

1. Make a diagram of the gutter runs.

2. Measure the length of each straight section of the gutter run and record the lengths [1,2] on the diagram.

Go to your material supplier and determine the lengths of the drop outlets [3,7] and mitered corners [4] you will be using.

3. Record the lengths of the drop outlets and mitered corners on the diagram.

4. To complete the diagram, subdivide each straight section of gutter run into 10 foot gutter length [6]. Determine other shorter length [5] needed.

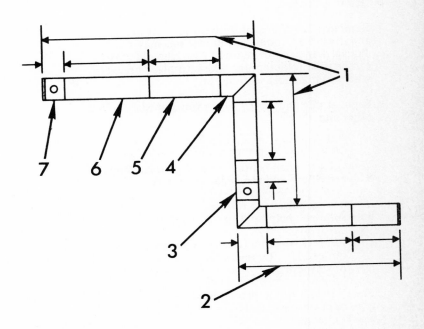

PREPARING TO REPLACE GUTTERS

Estimating Material

5. Use diagram to determine quantities of material needed. Record the information on the diagram.

   • Record number of inside [3] and outside [6] mitered corners.

   • Record number of drop outlets [2,7]. Drop outlets should be no more than 40 feet apart.

   • Record number of slip joint connectors. Connectors [9] must be used where a gutter section meets a mitered corner, a preformed gutter drop outlet, or another gutter section.

   • Record number of right [5] and left [1] end caps.

   • Record number of fasteners. You will need fasteners at both sides of a drop outlet and mitered corner, and at every 30 inches of gutter section.

   • Record the number of 10 foot gutter lengths needed. When two short lengths [4,8] of a gutter run are added together and the result exceeds 10 feet, each short length should be cut from a 10 foot section. This will avoid having to install two short lengths in a straight section of the gutter run.

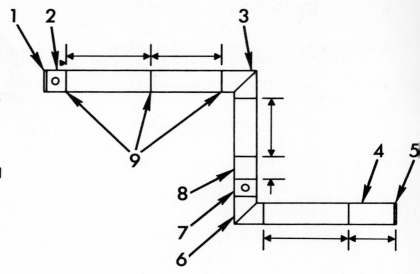

▶ **Remove Gutters**

Remove old gutters carefully to prevent breakage and distortion. Some gutter sections may not be damaged and can be reused. Also, the old gutters can be used to determine where to place brackets, where to use short sections, etc.

Begin at one end of the gutter run and work to the other end.

WARNING

Wear gloves when handling metal gutters. Metal edges are sharp and can cause deep cuts.

If removing gutter run of more than 6 feet length, have someone help hold the gutter sections.

1. Remove sheet metal screws on sides of drop outlet [1]. Remove straps [3] and downspout [2].

The next part of the procedure depends upon the type of gutter fasteners used. If your gutters have, **bracket hangers,** go to Step 5 **spike fasteners,** go to Step 9 **strap hangers,** continue with Step 2

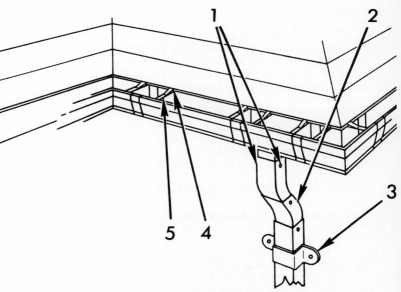

Strap hangers are nailed to the roof under the shingles. Do not try to remove the straps, since you might loosen the shingles and damage the roof.

2. Using tin snips, cut strap [5] of hangers at edge [4] of roof. Cut straps for only a few sections at a time.

3. Disconnect gutter sections from connectors [1] and remove gutter sections.

4. Repeat Steps 2 and 3 until all gutter sections are removed. Go to Step 15.

For **bracket hangers,** use Steps 5 through 8 to remove.

5. Disconnect or cut bracket hangers [6] for a few gutter sections. Remove bracket hangers from gutter sections.

6. Disconnect gutter sections from connectors [1] and remove gutter sections.

7. Carefully remove bracket hangers [8] from fascia board [7].

8. Repeat Steps 5, 6, and 7 until all gutter sections are removed. Go to Step 15.

For **spike fasteners,** use Steps 9, 10, and 11 to remove.

9. Place wooden block [3] inside gutter. Use block of about the same width as gutter.

10. Insert pry bar between spike head [4] and front of gutter [2].

11. Holding block in place, remove spike from fascia board. Remove spike and ferrule [5] from gutter.

12. Repeat Steps 9 through 11 for all spikes in section.

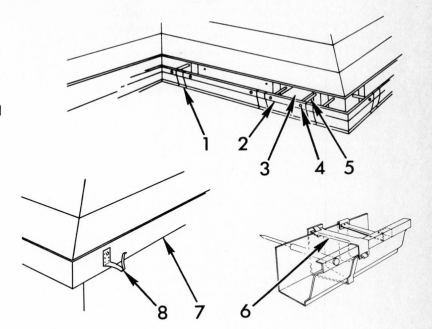

13. Disconnect gutter section from connector [2]. Remove gutter section.

14. Continue until all gutter sections of concern are removed. Continue with Step 15.

If fascia board [1] is damaged, replace damaged parts.

15. Check that fascia board [1] is not split, warped, damaged, or decayed.

16. Fill nail holes and small cracks in fascia board with wood putty.

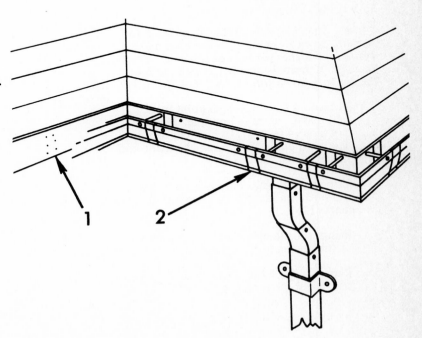

► **Mark Slope of Gutter Run**

For efficient drainage, gutters must be installed with a slight slope toward the downspout. Some gutters are installed with a slope as high as 1/4 inch per foot of gutter. However, a slope of 1/16 inch per foot of gutter is good enough for most cases.

Downspouts should be installed next to the outside corners of the house. One downspout is required for every 35 to 40 feet of continuous gutter. Gutter runs longer than 40 feet need two down-spouts, one at each end. When you need downspouts at each end of a gutter run, locate the highest point in the middle and let the gutter slope toward the downspout at each end.

1. Using marking pencil and rule, make a mark [2] on fascia board 1/2 inch below edge of eaves at highest point of a straight section of gutter run.

2. Using a straightedge 6 to 8 feet long and a carpenter's level, mark a level line [1] 5 feet long on the fascia board toward low end of gutter run.

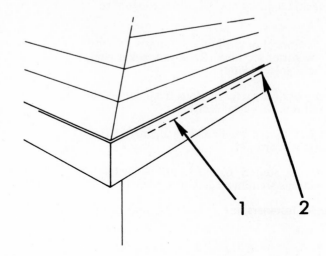

Instructions below show how to mark a slope of 1/16 inch per foot.

For any other slope the distance in inches to measure down from mark on the level line will be 4 times the inches per foot of slope desired. For example, if desired slope is 1/8 inch per foot, the distance down will be 4 x 1/8 which is 1/2 inch.

3. Measure 4 feet from high point mark [2] and make a mark [1] on line. Measure 1/4 inch (4 feet x 1/16 inch per foot is 1/4 inch) down from mark just made and make another mark [4].

4. Using straightedge and marking pencil, draw a line [3] on fascia board through the two marks [2,4].

5. Using straightedge, extend line [3] to end of straight section of gutter run.

6. Repeat Steps 1 through 5 to mark slope of all straight sections of gutter run.

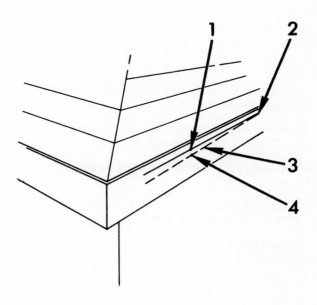

▶ **Assemble Metal Gutters**

Use diagram made earlier of old gutter runs as a guide to assemble gutters.

1. Start at one end of gutter run. Place pieces of one gutter run on ground in positions shown on diagram.

When determining exact length of gutter, include distance needed for connectors at each end.

2. Temporarily connect drop outlets, corners, and 10 foot lengths to determine exact lengths [1,2,3] of gutter sections less than 10 feet long needed to complete each straight section of gutter run. Record lengths on diagram for use later.

3. Measure and mark a piece of gutter to exact length needed. Using combination square, mark right angle cut lines on each side and bottom of gutter.

Cut enameled gutters with tin snips to prevent chipping. Unfinished gutters may be cut with tin snips or with a hacksaw.

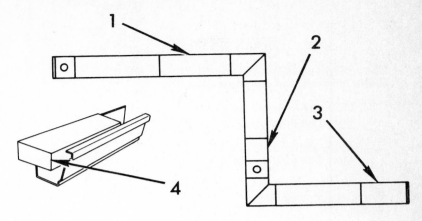

CAUTION

When using a hacksaw, place a 2 x 4 board [4] between walls of gutter near line to support gutter. If not supported, the metal will bend, be difficult to cut, and may be damaged.

4. Cut gutter along lines. Smooth cut edge by carefully filing off burrs and sharp corners. Apply a rust-preventive primer to cut edge.

Use Steps 5 through 8 below only if using spike and ferrule fasteners.

Mitered corners and drop outlets need two spike holes [1].

New spikes should not be driven into old spike holes in the fascia board. If using old gutter runs as a guide, locate spike marks 1 inch away from old spike holes.

5. Measure and mark spike locations on front lip [3] of gutter. Mark spike locations no more than 30 inches apart.

6. Use a clamp to hold 2 x 4 board [4] between walls of gutter to provide support to gutter.

Use drill bit with same diameter as spike.

7. Center punch and drill holes. Remove clamp and board.

8. Place spike through holes square with front lip [3] of gutter. Use spike to mark hole locations on back wall of gutter [2]. Remove spike.

9. Use clamp to hold 2 x 4 board between walls of gutters. Center punch and drill holes on back wall of gutter. Remove clamp and board.

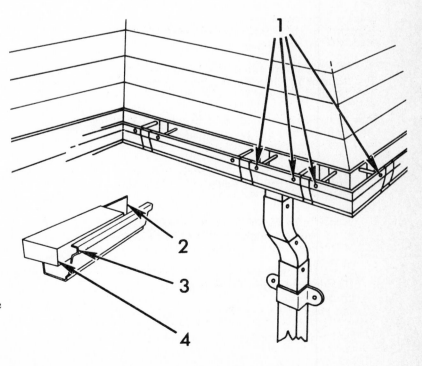

WARNING

Wear gloves when handling metal gutters. Metal edges are sharp and can cause deep cuts.

1. Place gutter pieces on ground in positions shown on diagram made earlier.

2. Apply gutter mastic to joints [1] of end caps. Install end caps [2].

An overly long section will place undue stress on connectors during handling. Keep a section within 10 to 15 feet long by using only one long piece connected with a short piece or with a drop outlet or a corner piece.

3. Apply gutter mastic to connector joints [4]. Assemble drop outlets [5], corners [6], and gutters [3] to form sections 10 to 15 feet long.

4. Place assembled gutter sections on ground in positions shown on diagram made earlier.

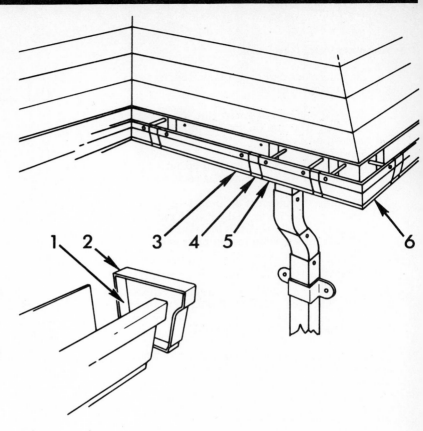

If using spike and ferrule fasteners, go to Page 95.

Bracket hangers should be installed not more than 30 inches apart. Mitered corners and drop outlets need two fasteners to support ends.

5. Starting at one end of gutter run, measure distance to where bracket hangers are to be installed. Record measurement on diagram.

Nails or screws should not be driven into old holes in fascia boards. Locate marks 1 inch away from old holes.

6. Using measurements from Step 5, mark location for bracket hangers on slope line [3] made earlier.

7. Temporarily install a bracket [2] on a gutter piece. Make a mark on edge [1] of **bracket** at top edge of gutter. Remove bracket from gutter.

8. Using combination square, make line [4] on bracket at mark. Use this bracket as guide and mark all bracket the same way.

9. Nail or screw bracket hangers at location marked on fascia board with line [4] on bracket aligned with slope line of gutter run.

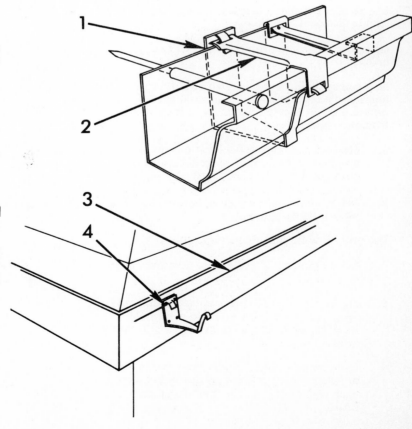

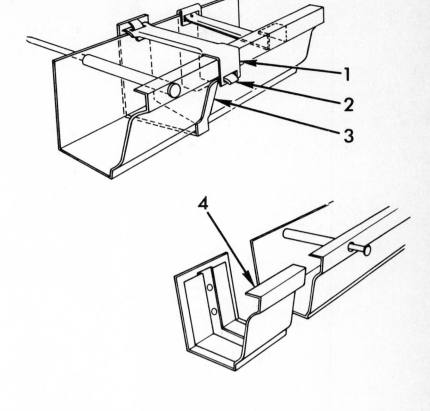

10. Start at one end of gutter run. Place first section on straps [3] of bracket hangers. Connect straps [1,3] of bracket hangers around gutter. Bend tabs [2].

11. Apply mastic to connector at end of section. Place next section on straps [3] of bracket hangers.

12. Place end of gutter section into connector. Bend lip [4] of connector against lip of gutter.

13. Connect straps [1,3] of bracket hangers around gutter. Bend tabs [2].

14. Continue until all gutter sections are installed.

Go to Page 96 to install downspouts.

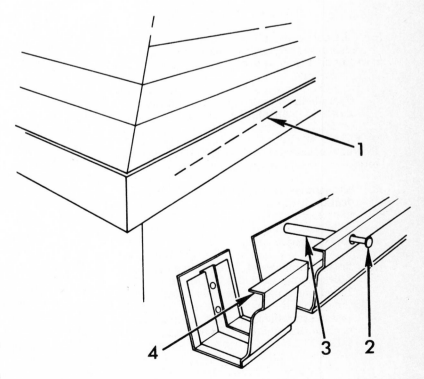

If installing gutters with **spike and ferrule fasteners,** perform Steps 15 through 20 below.

Use a helper to hold gutter section while installing spike and ferrules.

Read Steps 15 and 16 before starting. Be sure to start at one end of gutter run.

15. Place gutter section on fascia board with top of gutter section on slope line [1] made earlier.

16. Place spike [2] through hole in lip of gutter. Place ferrule [3] on spike. Align spike and ferrule with hole on back of gutter. Hammer spike into fascia board.

17. Repeat Step 16 until all spikes are nailed to fascia board.

18. Apply mastic to connector at end of section. Place end of next gutter section into connector. Bend lip [4] of connector against lip of gutter.

19. Repeat Steps 15 and 16 to nail gutter section to fascia board.

20. Continue until all gutter sections are installed.

▶ **Assemble Downspouts**

If roof has a wide overhang [2], use elbows [6] to reach wall of house.

If overhang is wider than connected width [1] of elbows, use a piece of downspout between elbows to reach wall of house.

1. Measure width of roof overhang [2].

2. Measure width [1] of connected length of elbows [6].

Downspout pieces are assembled by placing end of one piece [4] inside end of other piece [5]. Measured length [3] of pieces must include this distance.

3. Calculate length of downspout needed to reach wall of house.

4. Measure and cut piece of downspout to length [3] needed. Use file to remove burrs or sharp edges. Paint cut edge with rust preventive primer.

5. Install downspout piece between elbows [6].

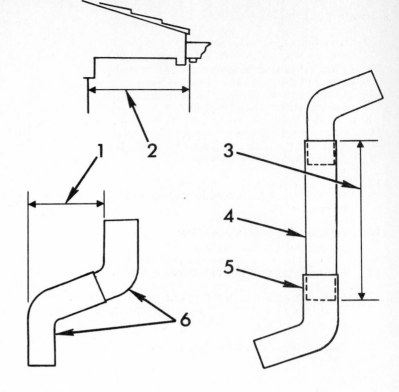

6. Drill two holes [2] in opposite sides of elbows where pieces join. Install sheet metal screws in holes to hold pieces together.

7. Install elbow in drop outlet. Drill two holes [1]. Install sheet metal screws in holes.

Downspouts should end at drain tile [7] or splash block [6] to direct water away from house.

8. Measure and cut downspout pieces [4] to length.

Assemble pieces of downspout before connecting to elbow or drop outlet.

9. Assemble pieces [4,5] of downspout. Drill holes in opposite sides where pieces join. Install sheet metal screws in holes.

10. Install assembled pieces of downspout to drop outlet or elbow. Drill holes in opposite sides [3]. Install sheet metal screws.

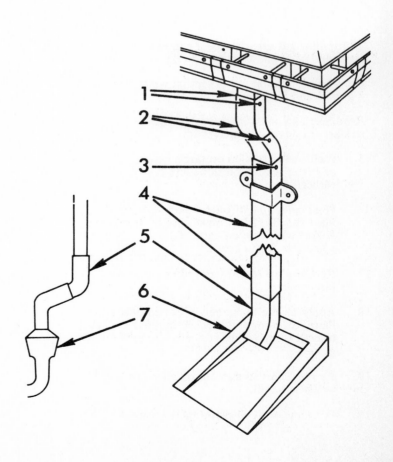

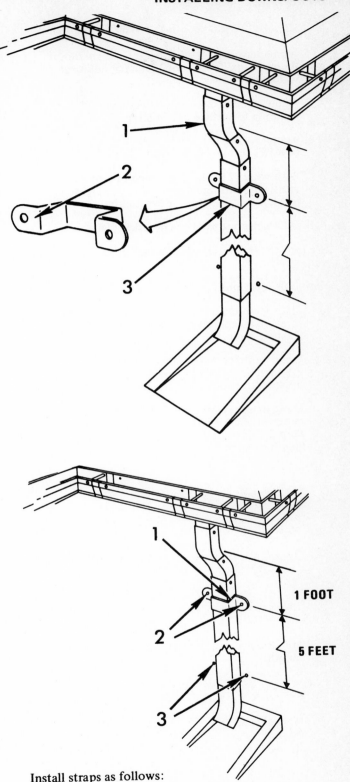

▶ Attach Downspouts

The downspout assembly is attached to wall of house with straps [3] spaced 5 feet apart. First strap should be installed 1 foot or less below elbow or drop outlet [1].

The method of attaching assembled downspout depends upon whether assembly is to be attached to a stucco, a stone or brick, or a wooden wall.

- Go below to **attach downspout to stucco walls.**

- Go to Page 98 to **attach downspout to stone or brick walls.**

▶ Attach Downspout to Wooden Walls

1. Apply approximately a 1/16 inch thick layer of caulking to surface [2] of top strap [3].

2. Place top strap [3] over downspout. Nail strap to wall using two 2 penny aluminum or galvanized nails.

3. Repeat Steps 1 and 2 to install remaining straps.

▶ Attach Downspout to Stucco Walls

In order to attach downspouts to stucco walls, drill holes through stucco material to:

- Determine if there is a wall stud.

- Use as a pilot hole for nails or for drilling larger holes for toggle bolts.

Mark hole locations for straps as follows:

1. Place strap [1] over downspout where strap is to be installed. Mark locations of holes [2]. Remove strap.

2. Using hammer and center punch, make hole [3] about 1/8 inch deep.

3. Using 1/16 inch masonry bit, drill holes at marked locations. Drill until you feel resistance after drill bit goes about 1-1/4 inches into the stucco or until bit goes all the way through the stucco.

If there is **no** wall stud for either side of strap [1], go to Step 6.

4. Apply about a 1/16 inch thick layer of caulking to surface of strap [1].

Install straps as follows:

5. Place strap [1] over downspout with strap holes [2] aligned with holes in wall. Place nonmetal washer on nail. Nail strap to wall with masonry nails about 2-1/2 inches long.

INSTALLING DOWNSPOUTS

Attach Downspout to Stucco Walls

6. Using masonry bit slightly larger than diameter [1] of folded wing, enlarge holes in wall made earlier.

7. Apply about a 1/16 inch thick layer of caulking to surface [4] of strap.

8. Remove wing [2] from toggle bolt. Insert bolt [3] through strap. Reinstall wing [2].

9. With wing [2] folded and near end of bolt, push wing through hole in stucco. Tighten toggle bolt [3]. Do not overtighten.

▶ **Attach Downspout to Stone or Brick Walls**

Use lead anchors to attach downspout straps to wall.

Mark hole locations for straps as follows:

1. Place strap over downspout where strap is to be installed. Mark locations of holes. Remove strap.

2. Using hammer and center punch, make 1/8 inch deep hole in stone or brick at marked locations.

3. Using masonry bit slightly larger than diameter of anchor [5], enlarge holes made in Step 2. Make hole 3/8 inch deeper than length of anchor.

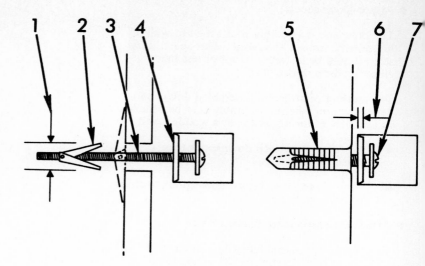

4. Install lead anchors [5] in holes.

Use screw [7] 1/4 inch longer than length of anchor plus thickness [6] of strap.

5. Place strap [6] over downspout with holes in strap aligned with holes in lead anchors. Install screw [7] in lead anchors. Tighten screw.

NOTES

NOTES